SNOWDONIA

160 pages of Ca

BEST V[ ]
WALKS

Editor: Llywarch ap Myrddin

First published in 2015

© original authors/Carreg Gwalch

© Carreg Gwalch 2015

All rights reserved. No part of this publication
may be reproduced, stored in a retrieval system,
or transmitted in any form or by any means, electronic,
electrostatic, magnetic tape, mechanical, photocopying,
recording, or otherwise, without prior permission
of the authors of the works herein.

ISBN: 978-1-84524-198-8

Cover design: Carreg Gwalch

Published by Gwasg Carreg Gwalch,
12 Iard yr Orsaf, Llanrwst, Wales LL26 0EH
tel: 01492 642031
fax: 01492 641502
email: books@carreg-gwalch.com
website: www.carreg-gwalch.com

Pont Gower, near Llanrwst, Conwy valley

Nant Ffrancon

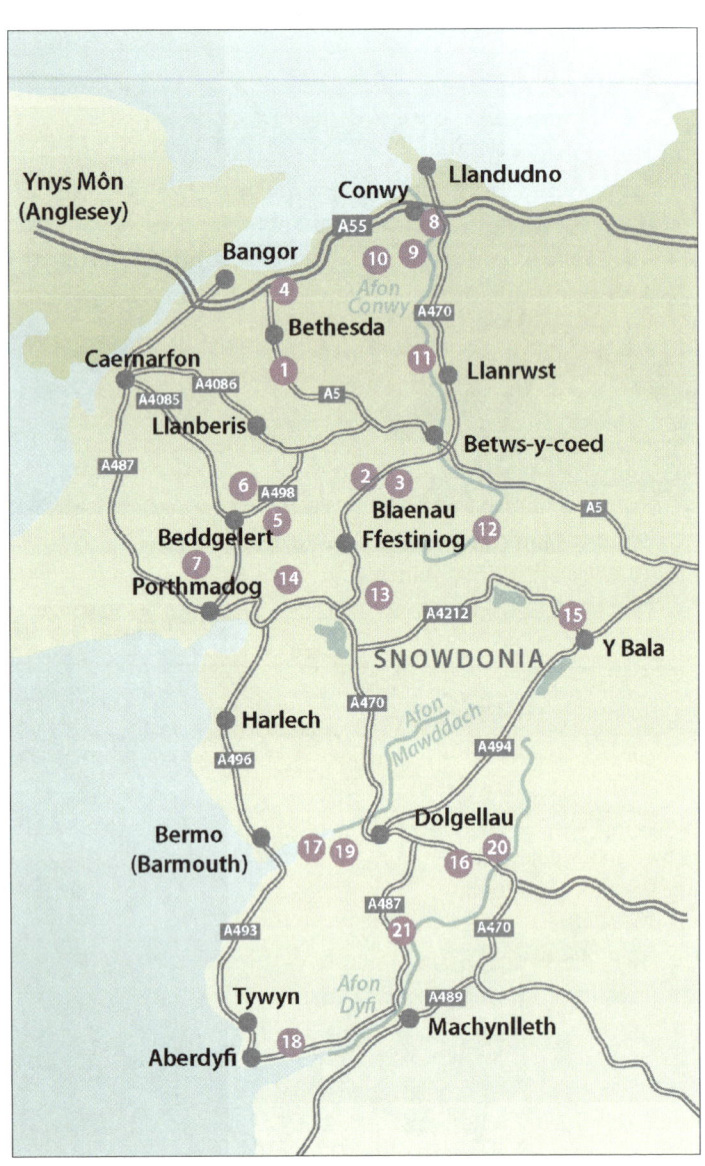

Contents

Central Snowdonia Valley Walks

1. Nant Ffrancon — 7
2. Lledr Valley, Dolwyddelan — 11
3. Cwm Penamnen, Dolwyddelan — 19
4. Aber Falls — 25
5. Beddgelert and Mynydd Sygun — 37
6. Cwm Llan, Llyn Dinas — 47
7. Cwm Pennant — 53

Conwy Valley Walks

8. Conwy RSPB Reserve — 59
9. Caerhun Church and Conwy valley — 69
10. Around Llanbedrycennin and Ro-wen — 79
11. Tu Hwnt i'r Bont, Llanrwst — 87
12. Ysbyty Ifan, upper Conwy valley — 97

Meirionnydd Valley Walks

13. Cwm Cynfal, Ffestiniog — 105
14. Cwm Croesor — 109
15. Afon Tryweryn — 113
16. Nant Maesglase, Dinas Mawddwy — 117
17. Mawddach Estuary — 123
18. Pennal, Dyfi valley — 133
19. Penmaenpool — 139
20. Cwm Cewydd, Dinas Mawddwy — 145
21. Aberllefenni, Afon Dulas, Corris — 153

Carreg Gwalch Best Valley Walks in Snowdonia

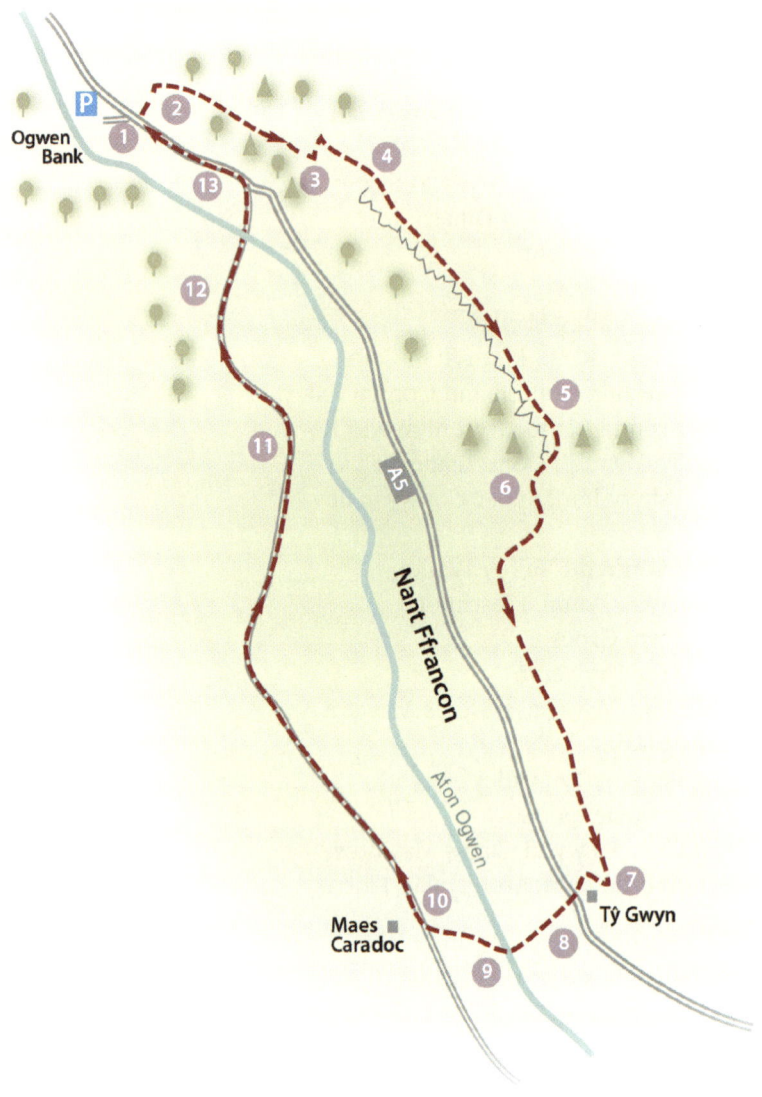

Walk 1
Nant Ffrancon

Walk details

Approx distance: 5½ miles/9 kilometres

Approx time: 3–3½ hours

O.S. Maps: 1:50 000 *Landranger Sheet 115*
1:25 000 *Explorer OL 17*

Start: *Lay-by just north of the turning to Ogwen Bank Grid Ref. SH 637 654*

Access: *About ½ mile south of the junction between B4409 and A5 (Bethesda/Betws-y-coed)*

Parking: *Park in a lay-by just north of the turning to Ogwen Bank.*

Going: *Short climb, gentle ascent and gentle descent; wet patch on final footpath.*

This walk gives fine views of the mountains on either side of this valley, without involving any mountain ascents. After a short climb in the lovely woods S of Bethesda, you reach open land on the E side of the valley, with spectacular views. The gentle ascent is followed by an equally gentle descent to a point about half way along the valley. After crossing, an easy return is made down the old road and a final footpath. This has a wet patch, and if this is too bad it is not much of a detour to end the walk along the A5, which has a pavement. Stage 5 may also be marshy after rain.

Walk directions

1. Go up the signposted path opposite the turning to Ogwen Bank.
2. Go through gate and turn R. After 300m fork R.
3. In the open the wide path turns sharp L. Go on towards forest, then turn R along a crossing track 80m before forest.
4. Pass fold (keep on your R) and, 100m later, fork R over grass to join path running near wall. Keep on your R.
5. Above wood, cross three streams and go through wall gap to stile. Cross stile and turn L along by wall. Keep on when fence turns L.
6. On meeting grass track bear L up it. It soon bears R to stile. Here, with your back to the wall, turn ½L and walk down grass 100m to join wide grassy path. Go L down it, soon joining main path (marked by rushes and a line of stones).
7. Above farm in pines, go sharp R down path to gate. There go L (with fence on your R) over drive to small gate.
8. Over road, through small gate and on to bridge.
9. Cross bridge and go ½R over fields to farm.
10. Turn R along road.
11. As road turns R to cross river, keep on along track. Keep on down to wall and bear L to walk beside it.
12. At farm, go R through farm gate and at once L through small gate. Soon on along track.
13. Go L along pavement at road.

Other paths:

The public path mapped through the wood (639 644) does not seem to exist. (The path I use near here is marked by arrows, indicating it can be used.)

Originally published in *New Walks in Snowdonia* by Don Hinson

At the head of Nant Ffrancon

Carreg Gwalch Best Valley Walks in Snowdonia

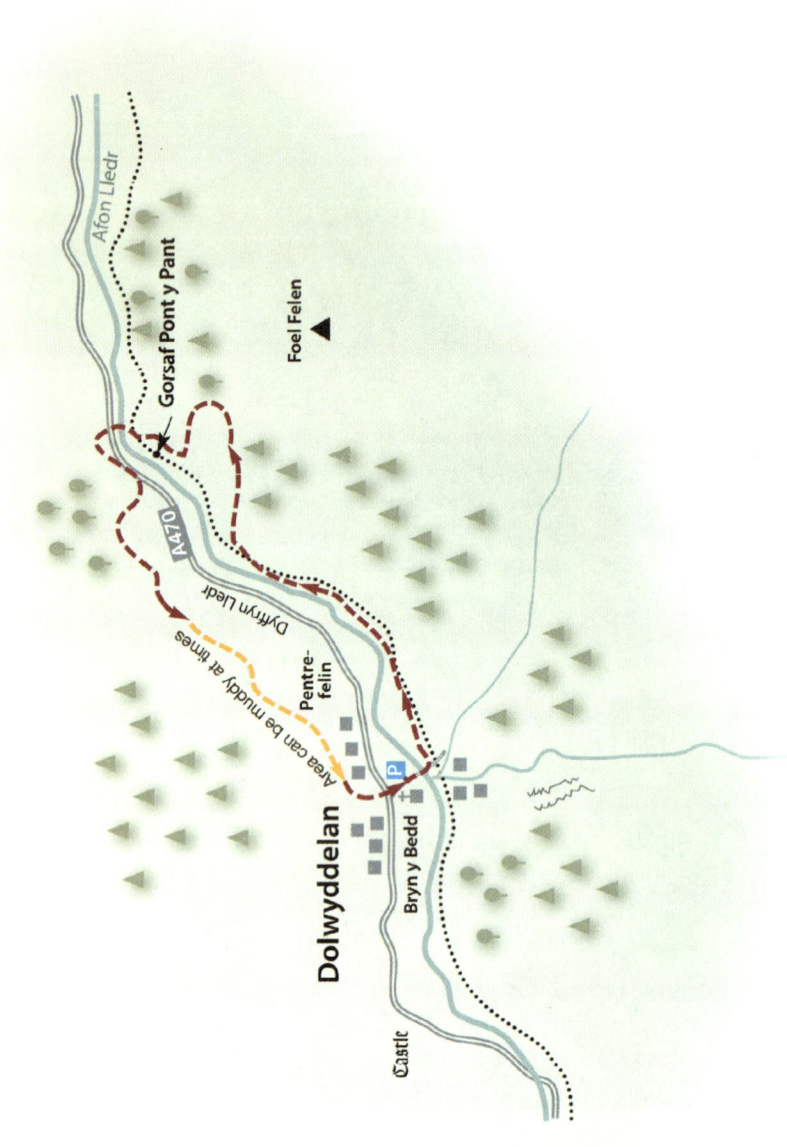

Walk 2
Lledr Valley, Dolwyddelan

Walk details
Approx distance: *4 miles/6.4 kilometres*

Approx time: *2 hours*

O.S. Maps: *1:50 000 Landranger Sheet 115*
1:25 000 Explorer OL 18

Start: *Dolwyddelan station*
Grid Ref. SH 738 522

Access: *Dolwyddelan by car, bus or train. There is a bus stop in the centre of the village and it is possible to park along the road to the station. Walk towards the station, or if coming by train, start the walk from the station.*

Parking: *Spaces at the station or roadside in village*

Going: *Riverbank and woodland paths*

The walk

From Dolwyddelan, along the banks of the river Lledr, past Pont y Pant station, then across the main road and back along a woodland path to Dolwyddelan.

You can reach Dolwyddelan by car, bus or train. There is a bus stop in the centre of the village and it is possible to park along the road to the station. Walk towards the station or, if coming by train, start the walk from the station.

Walk towards the station, past the parish church on

Elen's Castle Hotel, Dolwyddelan

the right and a memorial to those who died in both world wars on the left. Ignore the Public Footpath sign on the left. Proceed over the first bridge and then turn left between the school and the station. (If you came by train, this is where the walk starts.)

Proceed onwards along the road, through the gate and past Tŷ Isaf farm. Go through two more gates and along the road that runs along the banks of the river Lledr and to a sign and bridge on the left. Don't cross this bridge but go straight on, over a small bridge, through a gate and into a field. The path follows the wall and goes past a house on the right and then between a fence and woods. Walk under the railway and up to a gate. Go through the gate and follow the path through the woods and then down to a small white gate and a small gate.

Go through the small gate and then past a house and a cottage on the left. Walk straight ahead, ignoring a Public Footpath sign on the right. Pass two houses on the right – Caldy Villa and Cae Sarn – and on towards Pont y Pant station on the left. How about going onto the platform to have a look at the display board about the area's history?

Afterwards, return to the road and walk over a bridge, past the Plas Hall hotel on the right and over a bridge to the main road. Cross the road, carefully looking left and right, and go to a small gate. Go through it and walk up the path through the woods to a gate and stile. Go over the stone stile and walk to the left along the lane to the main road. Turn right and walk along the right hand side of the road, past a milestone and then on the right you'll see a Public Footpath sign and a lane going uphill.

Follow the lane through a farmyard and on through two gates, and then enter the field on the left. Look for a path going up to the left and follow it to a stile. Go over it and walk along the field to a track. Go left and then climb a stile on the right. Walk along the field following the posts to a stile. Go over it and follow the path through the woods, again following the posts, and you'll arrive at a stile. Climb over it and turn left following the path that runs alongside a fence.

Go on through pine trees until you reach a lane. Turn left and after a few metres you will see a road turning right. Follow it. Then look for a path going down to the left and follow it until you arrive at a narrow lane. Go down the hill to the left and you will come out at the main road.

Turn right and walk along the pavement past Elen's Castle Hotel, Moreia chapel and the Gwydir Hotel near

Dolwyddelan church

the bus stop. Cross the road and follow the sign to the station back to the car or train. If you came by car, how about visiting Dolwyddelan castle – one of the old castles of the Welsh? Drive in the direction of Blaenau Ffestiniog and the castle is about a mile from the village.

The story

Many long centuries ago, a large, ferocious animal plagued the people of the Conwy valley. It lived in a pool in the river near Betws-y-coed. This animal was a beaver, and it had amazing powers. When it was in a bad temper it would cause floods, destroying crops and drowning the cattle.

The area's bravest young men had tried to kill the beaver by throwing spears and shooting arrows at it, but these weapons did not break through its tough hide. The valley's wise men came together to reach agreement about what to do about the beaver. They

The 'dragon monster' carved on the ceiling of the church

decided to pull the beaver out of the pool and take it to one of the lakes up in the mountains.

Local blacksmiths forged large, strong chains of iron, and everyone went in search of the two strongest oxen in the area. Huw Gadarn owned the two strongest oxen, which had great long horns, and one morning he brought them to Betws-y-coed.

Before they could chain the beaver, it had to be lured out of its pool. After much head-scratching, one wise man remembered that the beaver liked pretty, young maidens. They looked for a brave young maiden who would be willing to try tempting the beaver out of its pool – and, at last, one was found.

The men and the two oxen went to hide in the woods near the beaver's pool and the maiden went to sit at the pool's edge and began to sing softly whilst combing her hair. Almost immediately an enormous pair of eyes surfaced, followed by a large head and then the rest of the monstrous beaver. The monster

Llyn yr Afanc ('the beaver pool') on Afon Conwy

emerged from the water and put its large, ugly head on the young maiden's lap and listened to her singing.

The men leapt from the woods and tied the beaver up in chains. This angered the beaver, and it smote the young maiden with its huge claws before leaping back into its pool. But the chains held firm and the oxen started to heave.

Step by step the beaver was pulled from the pool, along the riverbank and up the Lledr valley towards Dolwyddelan. Then, with all the men helping the oxen, the beaver was pulled through Bwlch Rhiw'r Ychen (*bwlch*: pass; *rhiw*: hill; *ychen*: oxen) and over Moel Siabod to the head of Nantgwynant. Such was their exertion that one ox's eye fell out, causing it to weep. The pool that was formed by the ox's tears has been known ever since as Pwll Llygad yr Ych (*pwll*: pool; *llygad*: eye; *ych*: ox).

The oxen pulled the beaver up Cwm Dyli and past Llyn Llydaw until, at last, they arrived at Llyn Glaslyn.

Dolwyddelan castle

At the lakeside, the men removed the chains. Once the beaver was free, it leapt into the lake and some say it remains there today.

Translation of original text from
Anturio yn Eryri

by Dafydd Meirion

Carreg Gwalch Best Valley Walks in Snowdonia

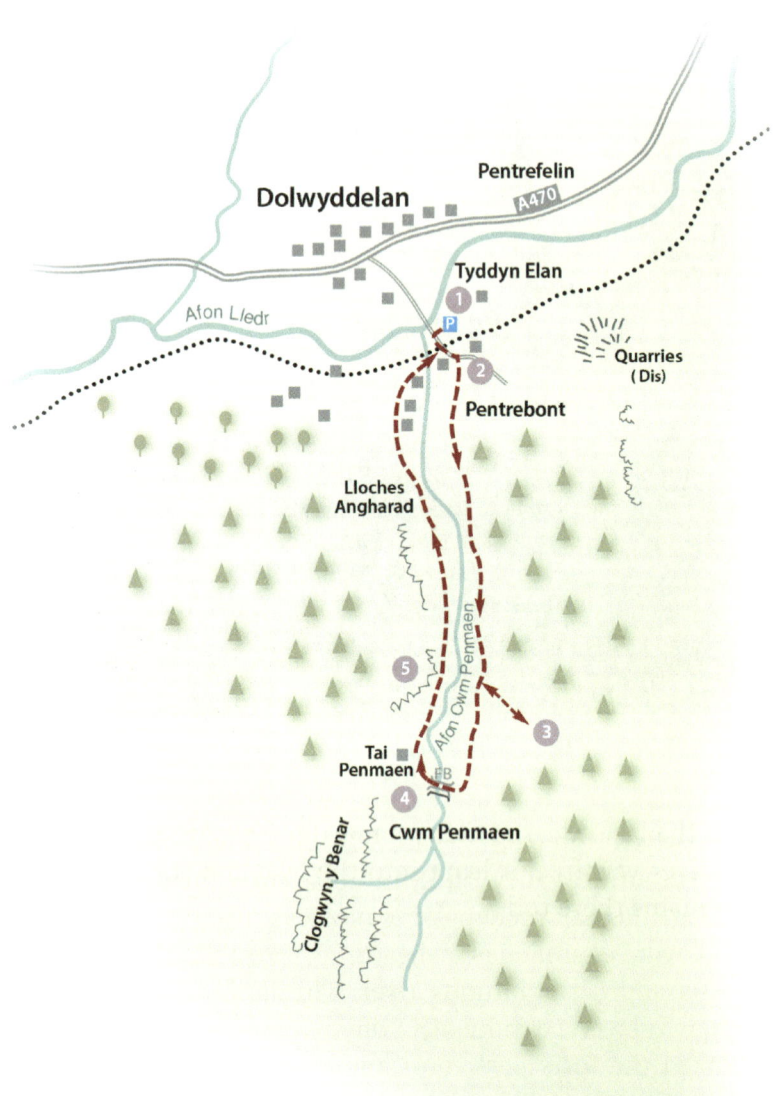

Walk 3
Cwm Penamnen, Dolwyddelan

Walk details

Approx distance: *2 miles/3.2 kilometres*

Approx time: *1 hour*

O.S. Maps: *1:50 000 Landranger Sheet 115*
1:25 000 Explorer OL 18

Start: *Car park beside Dolwyddelan railway station*
Grid Ref. SH 738 522

Access: *Leave the A5 for the A470 south of Betws-y-coed. At Dolwyddelan, take the road signposted to the railway station. Trains from Blaenau Ffestiniog, Llandudno and Llandudno Junction to Dolwyddelan (request stop). Buses from Blaenau Ffestiniog, Llandudno and Llandudno Junction to Dolwyddelan*

Parking: *Car park beside Dolwyddelan railway station*

Going: *Forest track and rural road*

This short, interesting walk follows a forest track into the beautiful valley of Cwm Penamnen then returns along a Roman road, passing medieval ruins.

Cwm Penamnen is a a beautiful, forested valley with cliffs and a tumultuous river. The lane through the cwm follows the route of a Roman road, Sarn Elen, that linked the forts between Canovium at Caerhun near Conwy with Moridunum at Caernarfon. The ruins of Tai Penamnen are being excavated and there is an information board about the site.

Cwm Penamnen above Dolwyddelan

The house once belonged to Maredudd ap Ieuan who was a tenant of Dolwyddelan castle. He built the present church in the village about AD 1500 and gave the tenancy of his cottages in the Lledr Valley to men with skills in archery. There was a gang of notorious bandits at Ysbyty Ifan over the hills to the south who terrorised the district. His force of over one hundred men brought about some degree of law and order.

Walk directions

1. From the car park walk out to the lane and turn left to cross the railway bridge. Bear left, ignore a terrace on the right and soon turn right along a track over a bridge.

2. Pass houses on the left and follow the rough track into the forest. If you look back you will have views of Moel Siabod and Dolwyddelan castle on its rock. Continue along the track, steadily uphill.

3. On reaching a track on the right with a white footprint sign, go right along it. You will soon have open views. The track goes downhill then levels out. Turn right at a signpost for Pont Carreg Alltrem and cross a wooden footbridge over Afon Cwmpenamnen.

The ruins of Tai Penamnen

4. Follow the path up to the lane where there are picnic tables and great views towards the head of the valley. Turn right along the lane and pass the remains of Tai Penamnen on both sides of the lane. Further on, go through a gate.

5. After a few metres, you can see a waterfall below on your right and, in places, the lane passes close to the river. Go through another gate and walk downhill past houses. Follow the road to the right and left over the railway lane to retrace your steps to the start

Originally published in
Short Family Walks in Snowdonia

by Dorothy Hamilton

Walk 4
Aber Falls

Walk details

Approx distance: 2¾ miles/4.4 kilometres
(Circular: 5 miles/8 kilometres)

Approx time: 1½ hours (3 hours)

O.S. Maps: 1:50 000 *Landranger Sheet 115*
1:25 000 *Explorer OL 17*

Start: *Grid Ref. SH 663 720*

Access: *From the A55 heading west, take the exit marked Abergwyngregyn. At the crossroads at the end of the sliproad, go straight across to the right of a workshop. At the next junction, turn right up a narrow lane through the village signposted to The Falls or Rhaeadr. After approximately 1 mile/1.6 km, you will reach a small parking area on the right of the lane before you cross the stone bridge. You can park and start your walk from here, but it may be easier to continue by car over the bridge and take a right turning up to the Forestry Commission car park. Here there are some picnic tables, and public toilets. In both cases, there is a parking fee, with proceeds going towards the maintenance of the area.*

If on the A55 heading east, take the exit marked Abergwyngregyn and pass under the A55. Turn right beside the workshop and follow the directions above.

Parking: *Forestry Commission car park – parking fee*

Going: *Gravel track with rocky footpaths and steps in parts on the main route to the falls. The path through the pine woodland can become muddy in places. Stony and grassy paths on the longer walk which are steep in places and can be slippery when wet.*

Site highlights:
- One of the area's great beauty spots
- Attractive valley walk set amongst the impressive Carneddau Mountains
- Dramatic 108 foot/33m high waterfall
- Woodland full of spring birds
- Stunning views along the coastline and across the Menai Strait to Anglesey
- Café in the village of Abergwyngregyn

Headline description

This is a very attractive walk up the wooded valley which bores its way into the Carneddau Mountains, culminating in the high Aber Falls. How impressive the flow of water is over the falls will depend upon the time of year of your visit, but the scenery is beautiful in any season. In spring, the areas of trees and bushes are alive with the sound of birdsong. More unusual migrants may be seen on the cliff face in season, while

Grey Wagtail

Aber Falls and lower valley

raptors can often be seen soaring overhead on thermals. This is a very popular venue at weekends, but by arriving early morning, you are likely to have peace and quiet on your walk. At peak times, the easy gravel path up to the falls can be busy, but if you choose to take the longer, circular walk, you will quickly lose any crowds and have the high hillsides to yourself.

Walk directions:
If you have parked by the roadside, go through the kissing gate to the right of the bridge and follow the path alongside the stream, going past the wooden carving depicting some of the wildlife that may be seen in the area.

As you walk alongside the stream, keep an eye open for Grey Wagtails and Dippers.

After crossing a wooden footbridge, you reach a gate onto a track. Turn right up the track, go right through the next kissing gate beside the interpretation board to continue up the valley towards the falls.

If you have parked in the car park, take the footpath next to the picnic tables which crosses the stream via a wooden bridge. Turn right and climb the steps until you reach a track at the top. Turn right and follow it downhill, climbing a stile halfway down. At the bottom of the hill, join the rest of the walk by turning left through the kissing gate beside the interpretation board.

This was a beauty spot popular with adventuring Victorians who waxed lyrical about the valley's picturesque qualities, as you can see in the display in the café in the village of Abergwyngregyn. As you walk along the track, check the trees and bushes around you for woodland birds, such as Nuthatches and Treecreepers, Coal Tits, Long-tailed Tits and Great Tits. You may hear Great Spotted Woodpeckers drumming in spring, and Jays calling in the trees. The valley rings with birdsong in spring, and in late April and May, you may hear Cuckoos calling.

Continue up the gently rising track, ignoring an alternative side path through the plantation, until you reach the cottage of Nant Rhaeadr.

This is a good spot to stop for a breather and to look back for views towards the Menai Strait. One of the cottage outbuildings houses a small visitor centre with information on the local area, its geology, flora and fauna, as well as a model of the surrounding landscape.

Continue up the gravel track, checking the trees and bushes for woodland birds as you go.

The majority of the valley is managed by the Countryside Council for Wales as a nature reserve, to encourage in spring birds such as Redstarts, Pied Flycatchers and Wood Warblers. As the waterfalls come into view, you reach the site of an archeological dig to the right of the track, identified as possibly being a Bronze Age Burial Site.

As the path becomes rockier, continue up until you reach the base of Rhaeadr Fawr/Aber Falls.

Rhaeadr Fawr/Aber Falls

Rhaeadr Fawr is the largest of three waterfalls here. At 108 feet/33m high, it is the highest in Wales, although the flow of water may be reduced after a dry spell in summer, and can even freeze in a severe winter. This is a good spot to see Grey Wagtails and, in spring, Black Redstarts and Ring Ouzels have been seen on the cliffs, while Buzzards and Ravens may soar overhead at any time of year.

Retrace your steps and cross the stream on the wooden footbridge to approach the waterfall from the other side.

On hot days, this can make a lovely picnic spot, with pools in the stream to keep feet, and bottled drinks, cool!

If you are looking for a shorter walk on fairly easy terrain, then you can retrace your steps to return to the car park. For a slight change to the route back, cross a stile on your right and take the path leading up across the scree slope towards the trees. Cross into the trees and follow the path through the dense woodland, keeping your eyes and ears open for Goldcrests as you walk through the conifers. Go through a kissing gate as you leave the pine woodland and continue downhill to rejoin the track. Retrace your steps to the car park.

However, if you want a longer, more challenging walk, with spectacular views along the way, you can cross the head of the valley here to see the other two waterfalls and then walk back along the hillside on the south side, returning to the car park via the village of Abergwyngregyn.

Having crossed the stream via the wooden bridge to view Rhaeadr Fawr from the south side, climb the ladder stile and follow the stony footpath to the two other waterfalls, Rhaeadr Bach (small falls) and Afon Gam. The steps down to the next footbridge are quite steep so take care here. Continue on the footpath past the waterfalls, and you will gradually lose the sound of falling water. Pick your way across several small streams before the path widens and becomes grassy for much easier walking.

From here you can look back down the valley through the gap between the hills to the Menai Strait. Around you in the bracken and gorse bushes, you are likely to hear the sounds of Stonechats and Wrens calling; look out for them perching on the tops of the bushes.

Continue along the grassy path, ignoring a ladder stile off to your left as the footpath bends round to the right to head back towards the coast. You will have to ford another stream here, but boulders make easy stepping stones across the water. The footpath generally follows the contour of the hill, with no steep rises or falls for a while. You can look across the valley to see where you walked up, and back behind you for a good view of the waterfalls. Not many visitors to Rhaeadr Fawr make it up to this point, and as you walk along on this south-east facing hillside, you can have all this exhilarating open space to yourself.

At a footpath sign, bear right leaving the track and head toward the ladder stile you can see in the distance. At this point the footpath and a stream share the same patch of ground so things can get a little boggy here. Cross the ladder stile and continue on the track going slightly uphill.

Meadow Pipits are common on the rough grassland here; look out for their distinctive song flights, climbing with rapid wing beats and then descending with wings and tail held stiff. Skylarks are also found here and you can enjoy a melodic serenade from above as they fly high in the sky. Ravens are often seen overhead, sometimes mobbing the Buzzards that also soar on the thermals. This is a great place to look down on a Buzzard circling below in the valley, an unusual perspective on a raptor.

Cross the next ladder stile and pass under the pylons which march rather incongruously over the Carneddau Mountains to the hydroelectric power station at Dolgarrog in the Conwy valley. Continue round the bend beside a stand of pine trees and climb over another ladder stile.

As you continue along the track, you will enjoy stunning views up and down the northern coast of

Wales: below you are the Lafan Sands, home to a thriving mussel industry in the clean waters here, and a chain of coastal nature reserves. Directly below you is Morfa Aber, with a car park, hide and small pool. Slightly to your right are the shallow pools and hides of Morfa Madryn, and the saltmarsh, and further right still is the promenade at Llanfairfechan, all excellent birding spots. Directly opposite you lies the black-and-white striped lighthouse on Penmon Point, Anglesey, and Puffin Island (Ynys Seiriol) just offshore. You can also see the attractive town of Beaumaris on Anglesey. Although the valley is defended by the mountains, it is also within reach of the sea-routes that enables close contact with Anglesey and the rest of Gwynedd's shores. No wonder the Welsh princes Llywelyn Fawr and Llywelyn ein Llyw Olaf used Aber as their stronghold, as shown in recent archaeological surveys.

The Welsh princes' township as seen from the motte at Aber

You may feel as if you are heading away from your destination but continue on the track past a metal barn and climb another ladder stile. Once over the stile, do not follow the North Wales Coastal Path sign for the path on your left. Instead, bear right and follow the track which starts to go downhill. You can now look down upon the village of Abergwyngregyn itself. Turn sharp right by a footpath sign to follow the path down towards the village. Do take care here, as this path drops quite steeply, and a stile halfway down the hill may control the sheep but does not make the walker's life any easier! After losing height very rapidly, the footpath brings you into the the village itself. Go through the metal gate and down some stone steps onto the lane.

If you feel in need of refreshment after this steep descent, turn left to walk about 55 yards/50 m to Caffi Hen Felin in the heart of the village. To return to the car park, turn right and walk back up the lane ¾ mile/0.4 km, and you will find the first parking area. As the road bends left to cross a stone

The motte at Aber

View looking east along the coastline

bridge over the river, go through a kissing gate to walk beside the water.

Once again, this is a good place to see Grey Wagtails and Dippers. You will pass an ornate wooden seat, carved with images of the wildlife seen in and around this area.

Continue along the footpath up some stone steps and cross the river by the wooden footbridge. Go through the gate and turn left, going through a metal kissing gate. Turn right and follow the lane back to the car park and your starting point.

What to look for ...
... in spring: If you are lucky you may see Ring Ouzels at the cliffs; Redstarts, Pied Flycatchers, Wood Warblers, Tree Pipits, Willow Warblers and Garden Warblers may all be seen in the wooded areas; Cuckoos may also be calling; look for Northern Wheatears in the more open areas.

... in summer: Meadow Pipits and Skylarks on the rough grassland of the hilltops.

... all year round: Grey Wagtails and Dippers on the rocks in the stream; Nuthatches, Treecreepers, Great Spotted Woodpeckers, Jays, and Common Crossbills in the woodland areas; Choughs, Ravens, Peregrine Falcons, Common Buzzards over the cliffs and high over the hillside; Stonechats and Siskins in the trees and bushes in the more open areas.

Where to eat:
Caffi Hen Felin (*the old mill*) is in the centre of Abergwyngregyn. This café serves drinks, hot and cold meals and snacks, and homemade cakes. Tel 01248 689454

Other information:
- Car park, picnic tables and public toilets
- Parking fee (£2 at time of going to print)

What other sights are nearby:
- Llanfairfechan Promenade, saltmarsh and Morfa Madryn nature reserve
- Aberogwen and The Spinnies nature reserve
- University town of Bangor
- National Trust Penrhyn Castle
- Historic walled town and castle of Conwy

Originally published in
Birds, Boots and Butties: Conwy Valley/Eastern Snowdonia

by Ruth Miller

Carreg Gwalch Best Valley Walks in Snowdonia

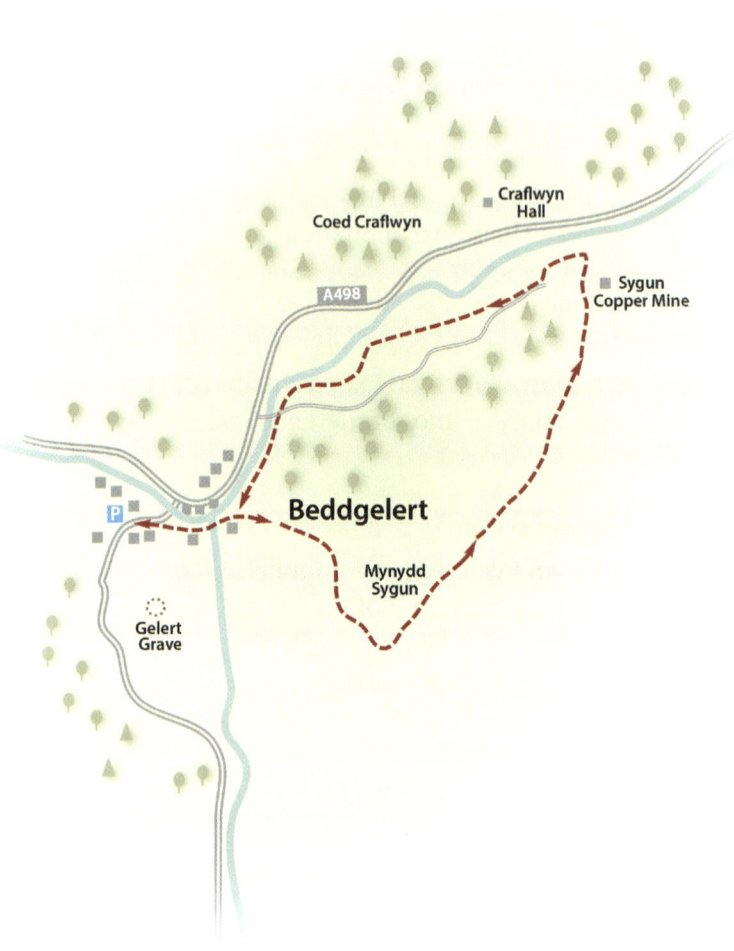

Walk 5
Beddgelert and Mynydd Sygun

Walk details

Approx distance:	6 miles/9.6 kilometres (not including visit to Sygun Copper Mine)
	1¼ mile/2 kilometres circular wheelchair route
Approx time:	3 hours
O.S. Maps:	1:50 000 Landranger Sheet 115
	1:25 000 Explorer OL 17
Start:	Tŷ Isaf (also known as Bwthyn Llywelyn), Beddgelert
	Grid Ref. SH 588 481
Access:	Park your car or come off the bus in the centre of Beddgelert and walk towards Tŷ Isaf near the Bridge
Parking:	There is a pay and display car park near the Information Centre in the centre of Beddgelert.
Please note:	The path is very steep in places and can be dangerous when descending from Mynydd Sygun (another route can be taken)
Going:	Some marshy ground

Bwthyn Llywelyn is a 17th century cottage, which contains an exhibition and small shop. There is a 1¼ mile circular wheelchair route along the riverbank past Gelert's grave.

The village of Beddgelert

The Walk – from Tŷ Isaf (Bwthyn Llywelyn) to the top of Mynydd Sygun, down to the Sygun Copper Mine and back to Beddgelert. The first part is steep but is well worth the effort for the spectacular views of the valley below and the Snowdonia Mountain range.

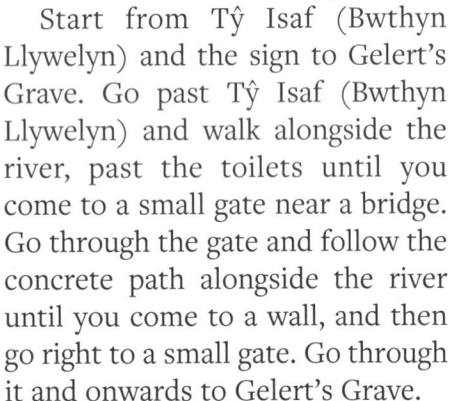

Start from Tŷ Isaf (Bwthyn Llywelyn) and the sign to Gelert's Grave. Go past Tŷ Isaf (Bwthyn Llywelyn) and walk alongside the river, past the toilets until you come to a small gate near a bridge. Go through the gate and follow the concrete path alongside the river until you come to a wall, and then go right to a small gate. Go through it and onwards to Gelert's Grave.

Retrace your steps back to the start of the concrete path and bridge. On your left is St

The riverside walk at Beddgelert

Mary's Church. Go over the bridge and straight ahead between two rows of houses and then left past the house at the end until you come to a public footpath sign. Walk up the hill until you reach Penlan on the left where Albert Bestall lived. There is a small gate in front of you. Go through it and up the steep rocky path until you come to a flat ridge.

Follow the footpath uphill to the right until you come to a gate in the wall. Go through it and follow the path to the right untill you come to a great view point near the summit of Mynydd Sygun. Here there are wonderful views of Beddgelert below as well as the river Glaslyn and its estuary and Bae Ceredigion in the distance. Then follow the path to the left until you come to the summit of Mynydd Sygun.

Look for a poorly marked path going away from Beddgelert and the direction you've come from. The path goes through rocks and then onto marshy ground with a white stone near it. There are traces footpaths

Looking back at Beddgelert from Mynydd Sygun

in all direction here, try and keep on the main path going away from the direction you've allready come from. You'll come to a rock looking down on marshy ground and an old ruin. There is a trace of a steep path going over it (dangerous in places), you can follow this path untill you get to a pile of stones. Alternativly you can go downhill to the right before going left past the ruin and back uphill to the pile of stones.

From the pile of stones keep to the right path avoiding the path going directly downhill. Follow the path past a sign near a ruin until you reach a junction, here you go left and downhill. You will then reach flat ground with a wooden fence and a bench on your left and iron bars on the entrance to an old mine on your right.

Go down the wide path with the wooden fence on the left, through the gate and into the Sygun Copper

The returning footbridge to Beddgelert

Mine where you can visit the mine or stop for some refreshments.

Leave the copper mine site and turn left down a track which runs alongside a wooden fence (there is a public footpath sign on the fence). Go through the gate and follow the lane past many houses until you reach a bridge near the main road, but go through a gate near the public footpath sign. Follow the path which runs alongside the river Glaslyn. Go through the small gate and proceed to another gate, follow the path going stright by thre riverside. Go over the bridge and back to Beddgelert.

Other Points of Interest
Alfred Edmeades Bestall (1892-1986), author and illustrator of Rupert Bear from 1935-1965, was a schoolboy at Rydal Mount in Colwyn Bay from 1904-1911. He stayed with his parents at Trefriw in the Conwy valley in 1912 and 1913, and during this time

visited Beddgelert for the first time. After the First World War he stayed almost every year at Penrhiwgoch, Nantgwynant, until he purchased his own cottage, Penlan, in 1956. He lived mainly in Surrey, but stayed at Penlan several times a year. In 1980 Penlan became his permanent home, until cancer prevented him living on his own, and he died peacefully at Wern Nursing Home in 1986, aged 93. He was born to missionary parents in Mandalay, Burma, in 1892. A drawing of the head of a mouse caught in a trap won him a scholarship to the Central School of Arts and Crafts in Birmingham. After de-mob from the First World War he began illustrating for publications such as Tatler, Eve and Punch. In 1935 he was asked to illustrate and write the Rupert stories for the Daily Express. This he did for 30 years and, even after officially retiring in 1965, he contributed to the Rupert Annuals until he was 90.

Beddgelert The picturesque mountain village started to develop in the late 1700s. Before then there were only trackways criss-crossing the area used by farmers, cattle-drovers and copper miners. In the late 1700s a new turnpike road was built from Caernarfon to Dolgellau, through Beddgelert. The present main road from Caernarfon closely follows this route and by 1796 there was also a new Beddgelert bridge. During the Napoleonic wars there was a marked increase in English visitors and artists to northern Wales and in 1803 the new Beddgelert (now Royal Goat) Hotel was built to accommodate them. The hotel manager, with local men, created Gelert's grave, and it has attracted visitors ever since. In 1805 another new turnpike road was built, going from Nefyn through Beddgelert and the Nantgwynant valley to join the main road at Capel Curig.

Beddgelert was soon frequented by climbers, walkers and artists and by the 1840s most of the terraced cottages and guesthouses along the Caernarfon and Capel Curig roads had been built. The part of the village between the Royal Goat Hotel and the church was mainly built in the 1900s, although Bwthyn Llewelyn may date to the late 1500s and Church Street to the early 1800s.

It was the 1860s before the terraces and guesthouses across the river Glaslyn were erected, and in the 1950s a new bridge gave vehicular access. A short-lived narrow gauge railway was built in the 1920s from Dinas near Caernarfon to Porthmadog through Beddgelert to transport slate and copper, but by the time it opened most of the mines and quarries in the area were closing. The line was bought by rail enthusiasts in the 1990s and opened from Caernarfon to Dinas in 1997, hoping eventually to reach Porthmadog.

Gelert's Grave Llywelyn I (Llywelyn Fawr – *the Great*) would come to Nantgwynant in summer to hunt. With his dogs he and his men would chase wild boar, deer and wolves up in the mountains. His favourite dog was Gelert, who not only would fight the fiercest of beasts but was also kind to children.

One day Llywelyn and his wife and followers had gone to hunt leaving their child in the care of the maid. But once she heared the sound of the horn up in the mountains, she left the baby in its cradle and went out for a walk. Llywelyn suddenly realised that Gelert was not with him. He was sure that something had happened to it and he decided to return home.

As they reached the palace, Gelert came out with his tail wagging, but there was blood on its face. Llywelyn rushed into the palace and found the cradle overturned with the bedclothes on the floor and no sign of the baby. He was certain that Gelert had killed him. Llywelyn pulled out his sword and plunged it into his faithful dog, killing it instantly.

Then Llywelyn heard a baby cry. One of his men picked up the cradle and there they saw the baby, unharmed. They picked up some of the bedclothes, and found a huge wolf, dead.

Llywelyn realised what he had done. Gelert had killed the wolf and saved his son. He carried Gelert's body to a nearby field and buried him before placing a mound of stones on his grave.

But there is no truth in this story. Beddgelert is named after Saint Celer. There is no grave there and the story was invented in the 19th century by the owner of the Royal Goat Hotel in order to attract more visitors to the village.

St Mary's Church The first people to settle in the area were Christian missionaries who probably arrived by sea around 700 AD and established a hermitage on the west bank of the Afon Colwyn. Their leader may have been Celer, whose grave later gave the village its name. This early Christian community was by 1200 famous for its holiness and hospitality to travellers. By 1230 the community was re-formed as the Augustinian Priory of the Valley of St Mary of Snowdon and the Welsh princes gave them lands and paid for the new stone priory church, parts of which can still be seen. Around 1200 the land north of the rivers Glaslyn and Colwyn had been given by Llywelyn Fawr to the Cistercians of

Aberconwy. After Henry VIII closed all the monasteries in the 1530s, the priory church was made the parish church of the new parish of Beddgelert. The crown owned the land but by 1600 had sold it to local Welshmen who divided it into various estates.

The present church consists of a nave and chancel from the 13th century, with a 19th century north transept and vestry on the site of an earlier aisle. The earliest masonry, of which the principal remains are the three light east window and the two bay arcade, date from around 1230.

Sygun Copper Mine In this 19th century mine, which is open to the public, there are winding tunnels and large, colourful chambers, magnificent stalactite and stalagmite formations and copper ore veins which contain traces of gold, silver and other precious metals. The beautiful countryside captured the imagination of movie makers, who turned the mountainside surrounding Sygun into a Chinese village in 1958 for the filming of *The Inn of the Sixth Happiness*, starring the late Ingrid Bergman.

Originally published in
National Trust Walks
1. *Northern Wales*

by Dafydd Meirion

Carreg Gwalch Best Valley Walks in Snowdonia

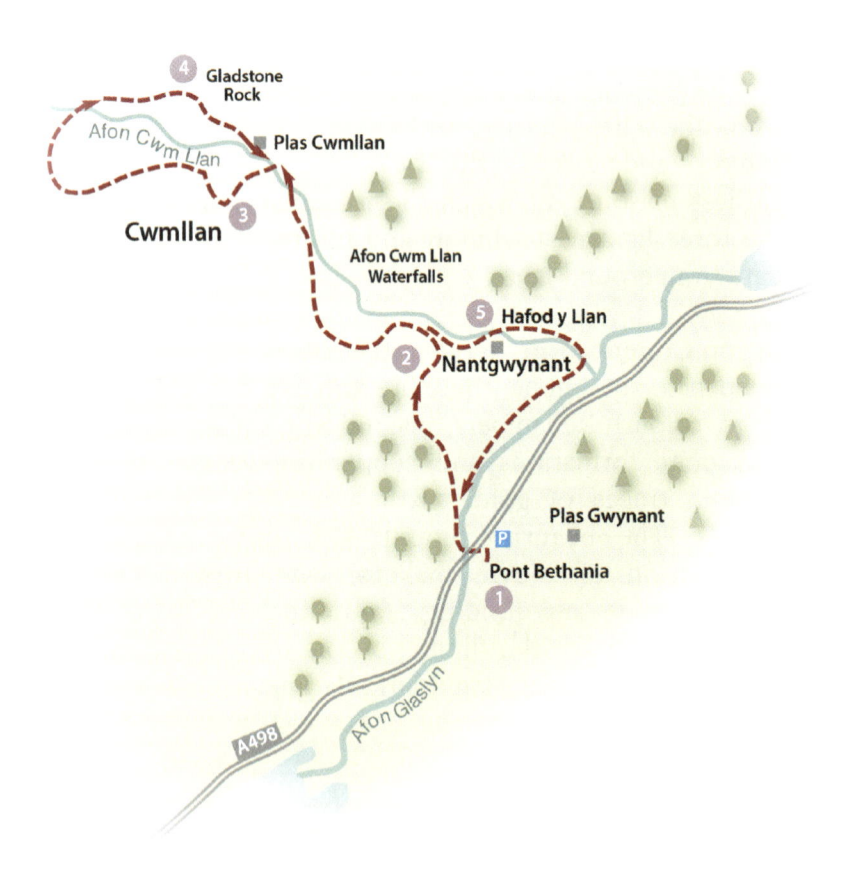

Walk 6
Cwm Llan, Llyn Dinas

Walk details

Approx distance: 5 miles/8 kilometres

Approx time: 3 hours

O.S. Maps: 1:50 000 *Landranger* Sheet 115
1:25 000 *Explorer* OL 17

Start: Pont Bethania car park in Nantgwynant
Grid Ref. SH 627 505

Access: A498 Beddgelert/Penygwryd

Parking: Car park on the A498 between Llyn Dinas and Llyn Gwynant

Please note: *Steady climb at start of walk*

Going: Moderate
Hill, woodland and riverside paths

Cwm Llan makes a fine destination for those who do not want to walk all the way to the summit of Yr Wyddfa (*Snowdon*). This half-day walk on the Watkin Path, passing the impressive waterfalls of Afon Cwm Llan, should not be missed. The route goes through land belonging to Hafod y Llan farm which was purchased by the National Trust in 1998 following a successful public appeal. The estate's land extends to the summit of Yr Wyddfa.

Early in the walk, you will pass the site of Sir Edward Watkin's chalet. Built in the 1890s on the site

The path at Cwm Llan

of an old cottage, the building had its own supply of electricity powered by Afon Gorsen. Sadly, the chalet was destroyed at the end of the 1939-1945 war after being occupied by the army.

The Watkin Path was built in 1892. Sir Edward Watkin, Liberal MP, brought William Gladstone, who was Prime Minister at that time, to Cwm Llan to open the path for public use for ever. Over 2,000 people gathered around a temporary, wooden platform on a rocky outcrop, the Gladstone Rock, to hear his speech on 13 September 1892. Several Welsh choirs were present and Mr Gladstone much enjoyed the hymns.

As you follow the track uphill past the waterfalls you will go through a cutting that was part of a tramway for the Hafod y Llan (Snowdon) quarry. It ended at the road near Pont Bethania and from there the slates were transported by horse drawn wagons to Porthmadog. In the 1870s there were hopes of a railway line in the valley, but it never arrived.

On the far side of Afon Cwm Llan are old copper workings and the remains of a mill, wheel pits and dressing floors where the copper was crushed before being sold in Liverpool and Swansea. The walk then takes the Braich-yr-Oen coppermine's tramway uphill to meet the level slate mine's tramway, which it follows through cuttings to the derelict buildings of the Hafod y Llan slate quarry. The slate quarry operated from the 1840s to the 1800s. You can see the remains of workshops and dressing sheds. Near the Watkin Path are the barracks where the workers lived during the week, although they went home at the weekends. Between here and the Gladstone rock, the Watkin Path goes along the slate quarry's original tramway. Just beyond the rock, you will pass Plas Cwmllan, the slate quarry manager's house. It was used for commando training during the 1939-1945 war and bullet holes can still be seen in the walls.

Walk directions

1. From the car park, cross the bridge over the river to the main road. Bear left and, in a few metres, turn right on a lane. Immediately, leave the lane to go up steps to a small gate. Follow the path through the wood and, at a track junction, bear left through a gate.

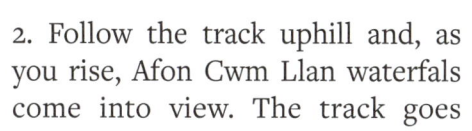

2. Follow the track uphill and, as you rise, Afon Cwm Llan waterfals come into view. The track goes

around left and right bends to reach a gate above the river. Continue along the path until it stops rising then bear left on the path that was the Braich-yr-Oen tramway.

3.   The path goes uphill to meet a level tramway. Turn right along it and follow on a level gradient untill you get to the slate quarry's ruined buildings, cross a bridge over the river. Bear right on a path to join the Watkin Path just below the slate quarry's barracks. Turn right and you will soon see the Gladstone Rock with its plaque on your right.

4. Further on along the track, you will pass the derelict Plas Cwmllan. Cross the bridge over Afon Cwm Llan and follow the Watkin Path downhill for about one kilometre going through a gate and past the main falls. Just after the right bend, look closely for a path on the left descending towards the river. Follow it downhill to a gate in the wall, and, further downhill, turn left through a gate. Bear right to walk through a camping field and, after passing through a gate, turn left over a bridge (not the first footbridge on the left).

5. Walk through a long field following a track through a gap in a wall. Just before reaching next gap in a wall along the track, turn right through a field following the river. Go through a gap in a wall to a footbridge. Bear left and follow the path beside Afon Glaslyn to a footbridge and lane. Turn left through a gate at a cattle grid to the A498 and car park.

Originally published in
Circular Walks around Beddgelert

by Dorothy Hamilton

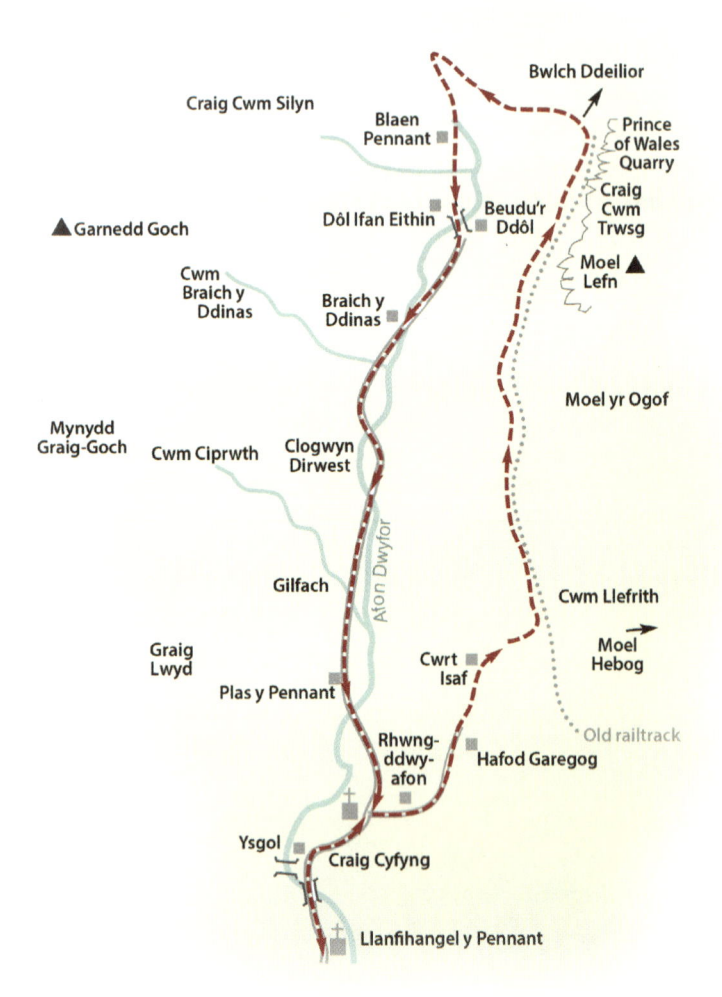

Walk 7
Cwm Pennant

Walk details

Approx distance: 8 miles/13 kilometres

Approx time: 3 hours

O.S. Maps: 1:50 000 *Landranger Sheet 115*
1:25 000 *Explorer OL 17*

Start: *Llanfihangel-y-Pennant church*
Grid Ref. SH 526 451

Access: *Take the A487(T) from Porthmadog to Caernarfon and between Penmorfa and Bryncir, take the country road to the right, marked 'Cwm Pennant'. Passing an old castle motte at Dolbenmaen and several farms, in about 2 miles you will arrive at the old church of Llanfihangel-y-Pennant on your right hand side.*

Parking: *Park by the church, or on the bend at Pont Cyfyng (the bridge)*

Going: *Clear, dry paths; tarmac road to return*

A fresh view awaits you around each bend along this meandering valley bottom road, as if the magician of the mountain discloses his treasures a few at a time. Cwm Pennant is featured often in Welsh literature – this pastoral landscape has made it especially popular with the Romantic Welsh poets. But underneath the centuries of agriculture, some industrial heritage can be found and the remains of slate quarries and copper mines are hidden beneath the green vegetation.

The church of Llanfihangel-y-Pennant by Pont Cyfyng

Walk directions

Cross over Pont Cyfyng – the bridge that crosses the river – and uphill past the old school. This walk is on the level mostly, but there is a chance to stretch the limbs on this small climb.

Turn right by the chapel, the road climbing upriver along the banks of Afon Cwm Llefrith – this foamy, cascading river is well described as a 'milky' river in its name. Passing Rhwng-ddwy-afon, the first farm on your left, you will notice that it lies on land between the two rivers of Ceunant-y-ddôl and Afon Cwm Llefrith.

The next farm – on the right – is called Hafod Garegog and is connected to a fairy tale. The old woman of Hafod Garegog was pestered daily by the 'fair folk', which are known by everyone to be living in this area – they wanted to borrow this and that day in day out. Losing patience with them, she said one morning, 'Yes, you can borrow it if you allow me two

The beauty of Cwm Pennant

wishes – that the first thing I touch will break and the second will stretch half a yard'. In her mind were the awkward stone which stuck out on her way to the door and the flannel jerkin that was half a yard too short in the kitchen. Unfortunately, she tripped on her way to the door and she clutched her thigh – which snapped like a dry twig. In her pain, she put her hand to her face, and touched her nose – which instantly grew half a yard.

On reaching the third farm, Cwrt Isaf, you reach the end of the tarmac road. Climb over the stile on your right towards the outbuildilngs and follow the old track up the slope until you reach the old tramway route – part of the evidence of the industrial heritage of this cwm. The tramway was worked between 1875 and 1894, carrying slates from the upper quarry to Gorseddau, Cwm Ystradllyn and onwards to Porthmadog harbour.

In front of you, there is a ridge of mountains – Moel Lefn, Moel yr Ogof and Moel Hebog. The uphill path would take you to Cwm Llefrith and through the pass to Beddgelert, passing Owain Glyndŵr's cave. Rare Alpine plant and the exceptional Killarney fern are found on the northern slopes.

The walk is now level and pleaseant, with wonderful views. Onwards, you cross many well-crafted bridges over small brooks, which can be torrential in high flood. When the high valley of Cwm Ciprwth opens in front of you, some copper mining scars can be seen on the landscape – dating back to 1828. An old water wheel from Truro, Cornwall can still be seen here.

Eventually you will reach the ruins of the old quarry mill at Prince of Wales quarry at the head of Cwm Pennant. In its heyday in 1870, 200 workers made a living here.

Cross over to Cwm Dwyfor, keeping on the same contour and passing another copper mine, Blaen-y-Pennant. The remains visible today are three lines of stone pillars between the shaft and the water wheel, which supported the timer trough carrying water and the winding gear. Some distance further you will find the old powder hut and, westwards, the barracks. Two hundred yards of tramway was built to reach an incline that dropped down to an extension of the road quarry tramway. This is your route to reach the river at Blaen Pennal.

The road will take you on the return journey to the bridge and the church, keeping true to the river's course all the way. Many come to these banks for picnics and bathing, others to fish, and some for peace and quiet.

Afon Dwyfor in Cwm Pennant

If you have the time, it is well worth calling at the graveyard. On the stones, past lives of shepherds, quarrymen and young men killed in a world war in France are recalled in fond memory – these are the people who have given this special cwm its wealth of heritage and history.

Walk 8
Conwy RSPB Reserve

Walk details

Approx distance: *2 miles/3.2 kilometres*

Approx time: *1½ hours*

O.S. Maps: 1:50 000 *Landranger Sheet 115*
1:20 000 *Explorer OL 17*

Start: Grid Ref. *SH 797 773*

Access: *From the A55 North Wales Expressway heading west, take the exit for the A547 signposted Conwy. This junction is marked with a brown 'RSPB Reserve' sign. Take the first exit left off the roundabout and follow the slip road downhill, bending sharp left at the bottom into the RSPB Reserve car park. Do not cause congestion by parking at the bottom of the hill by Afon Conwy.*

If you are heading east on the Expressway, ignore the first exit marked A547 for Conwy, continue on the A55 through the tunnel and take the next exit shortly after the tunnel for the A547 and Conwy. This is also marked with a brown RSPB Reserve sign. Turn right taking the third exit off the roundabout and follow the slip road into the RSPB Reserve car park.

Parking: *RSPB Reserve car park.*

Going: *Level, easy walking on gravel paths and boardwalks*

Site highlights
- Significant number of bird species all within a compact area

- Easy walking and comfortable hides provide excellent birding
- Spectacular scenery all around with the Carneddau mountains, scenic Conwy valley and historic walled town, and Conwy castle as a backdrop
- On-site RSPB Visitor Centre, Shop and Waterside Coffee Shop

Headline description

With its variety of habitat ranging from shallow lagoons fringed by reedbeds, and grassland and wild shrubby areas, to the mudbanks of Afon Conwy, this RSPB reserve attracts an impressive variety of birds and other wildlife, given its compact size. Although created as a result of building the A55 tunnel, you can quickly tune out any traffic noise and concentrate on the wildlife spectacle played out against the stunning backdrop of the Carneddau Mountains in the Eryri/Snowdonia National Park and the Conwy valley, with views of Conwy castle being the icing on the cake. The picture windows of the RSPB Waterside Coffee Shop overlook the first lagoon, so that in bad weather you can even enjoy birding without the risk of any storms in your teacup!

Walk directions:

From the car park, go through the Visitor Centre to access the reserve.

Check the board in the Visitor Centre to see what birds have been seen that day: an average day will provide around 65 species! You can also pick up a trail guide to the reserve, as well as special activities for children. Binoculars are available for hire. Guided walks and other events are organised throughout the year. As well as information on the reserve and its wildlife, the

Visitor Centre also includes an RSPB shop offering bird-related items such as field guides, outdoor clothing, binoculars and telescopes, bird food and gifts.

Leave the visitor centre and bear left following the trail into the reserve, passing the Waterside Coffee Shop as you do so.

View of lagoon and Conwy castle

If the weather is too bad to walk any further, the cafe has panoramic views over the first lagoon, allowing you to watch birds and enjoy your butty at the same time! Look out for waders including Black-tailed Godwits, Dunlins, Redshanks and Common Sandpipers, keeping an eye out for any rarities that may also drop in. An unusually confiding Water Rail is seen here regularly in the winter months, picking its way along the edge of the reeds right in front of the Coffee Shop.

Keep right, following the wooden boardwalk through the reeds. Turn right at the end and then turn right again at the next junction, and continue straight ahead to the Tal y Fan hide. This is a double hide giving excellent views over both lagoons, as well as a spectacular panorama back towards Conwy castle.

The reserve was created in 1995 as a result of digging

the A55 tunnel under Afon Conwy. Sludge from the tunnel diggings was dumped on this site, which, despite its inauspicious appearance, was leased by the RSPB who saw its potential as a nature reserve. Although this is a fairly young landscape, the reserve is now well-established. Islands created in the lagoons provide nest sites, feeding and roosting areas, while reed beds have grown up to provide cover around the water's edge. The habitat is managed carefully to benefit the numerous wildlife species jam-packed into this 48-hectare site: over two hundred species of bird have been recorded, as well as around four hundred plant species. Scanning the lagoons should provide a good selection of duck and waders, such as Oystercatchers, Curlews and Redshanks, Shelduck and Tufted Duck, and Wigeon, Teal and maybe Goldeneye in winter, as well as small birds such as Reed Buntings in the surrounding reed beds. In spring/summer, you may see Grey Herons and Little Egrets nesting in the

View of lagoon and coffee shop

Drake Tufted Duck

trees across Afon Conwy. On fine winter days, look out for soaring birds of prey: Buzzards may circle overhead, while in late winter afternoons, a Peregrine may lurk, hoping to snatch a meal from the massing flocks of Starlings that roosts overnight in the reeds here.

Retrace your steps back to the first junction and turn right, signposted Discovery Trail. Pass a picnic table and cross the wooden bridge over a pool. Pass through a kissing gate and turn right.

Look out for Welsh ponies grazing in this area in winter. These animals are utilised to keep the grass levels down in a manner that is sympathetic towards other plants and wildlife to maintain the biodiversity on the reserve. Rabbits are often seen, but the early walker may be lucky enough to catch a glimpse of a stoat, weasel or even an otter at the Reserve. In spring, many of the banks and verges are dotted with the nodding heads of Cowslips, while slightly later in the year, the amazing Bee Orchid appears. Look out for the incredible flower shape of this plant which mimics a bee.

Go through a second gate to the Carneddau Hide.

This hide overlooks the second lagoon, providing a closer look at its eastern bank. The islands provide nest sites in season for many species, particularly Lapwing. In spring, you can enjoy the Lapwings performing their tumbling display flights and bubbling calls as the breeding pairs establish their bond. The hide also provides a spectacular view towards the hills within the Eryri/Snowdonia National Park. At high tide on Afon Conwy, the wading birds are pushed off the estuary mudflats and move onto the islands in the lagoon, so the Carneddau Hide is the best spot to watch these birds such as Curlews, Oystercatchers and Redshanks.

Bee Orchid

Retrace your steps through the gate. Don't turn left at the first junction, as this will take you back the way you have come but carry on straight ahead, following signs for the Discovery Trail again. When you reach a T-junction, you can opt to take a short cut back to the Visitor Centre by turning left along the Discovery Trail and returning to the start of your walk through the Wildlife Garden.

Alternatively you can decide to take the longer walk to boost your bird list, which will take you to more viewing points, and alongside the Conwy estuary back to the Visitor Centre and car park. To take this route, turn right at the junction and follow the track as it bends to the right. Follow the track all the way to the corner, where you have an extensive view of the Conwy valley and at low tide, the river mudflats in front of Glan Conwy village.

As well as birds, the protected habitat of this reserve also provides a haven in season for butterflies, including the Painted Lady and the Clouded Yellow, Comma and Brimstone, and Cinnabar and Six-spot Burnet Moths.

Bear right to the viewing screen to see any birds that may be lurking in this quiet corner of the lagoon, then go through a kissing gate onto the estuary track, to shortly reach a second viewing screen.

As you walk along the estuary you are surrounded by spectacular views. Upstream to your left are the open uplands of the Carneddau Mountains. Downstream to your right lies the historic walled town of Conwy and the majestic thirteenth century Conwy castle, built by Edward I, as well as Isambard Kingdom Brunel's railway bridge dating from the 1800s. At low tide, a large expanse of mudflat is exposed along the shoreline, popular with duck such as Shelduck and Wigeon, as well as waders including Redshanks, Curlews and Oystercatchers.

Continue along the track until you reach the Benarth Hide on your right.

This hide overlooks both lagoons, and with the gently shelving shoreline right in front of it, can give excellent views of waders such as Black-tailed Godwits, as well as more elusive birds such as the Water Rail. In autumn and winter this is perhaps the best place to catch a flash of brilliant blue and orange as a Kingfisher passes.

Continue along the track, and on reaching the gate at the end, turn right to return to the car park, Visitor Centre and Waterside Coffee Shop.

What to look for . . .

. . . in spring: Lesser Whitethroats may be glimpsed in the scrubby bushes beside the path; Lapwings nest on the islands in the lagoon and make their swooping display flights; Grey Herons and Little Egrets feed on the lagoons as well as roosting and nesting in the trees across the Conwy estuary.

. . . in summer: The scratchy calls of Sedge and Reed Warblers should resound from the reedbeds and scrub, and you might catch a glimpse of the birds themselves; Common Whitethroats sing from the bushes beside the paths close to the hides.

. . . in autumn: Migrating waders pass through here: look for Black- and Bar-tailed Godwits on the lagoons, and possibly more unusual birds such as Curlew Sandpipers and Little Stints. Conwy RSPB has an amazing track record for turning up major rarities, so you never know your luck!

. . . in winter: Wigeon and Teal can be seen on the estuary mudflats depending on tide levels, and on the lagoons together with Goldeneye and Pochard; Starlings gather in great numbers at dusk forming swarms in the air over the lagoons, before swooping down into the reedbeds to roost for the night, while Peregrines loiter in the area looking for an easy meal; Water Rails can be seen at the edge of the reedbeds right in front of the Waterside Coffee Shop; given the ease and comfort with which you gan get unusually good views here of this normally secretive bird, this has got to be the best place in the UK to watch Water Rail.

. . . all year round: Finches and tits and even Reed Buntings visit the feeding stations around the Reserve; Grey Herons and Little Egrets can be seen fishing in the lagoons or out on the estuary; Shelducks and gull species gather on the exposed mud at low tide in the estuary and move on to the lagoons to join the resident Mute Swans and Tufted Ducks.

Where to eat:
The RSPB Waterside Coffee Shop serves hot and cold drinks, snacks, including home-made cakes and light meals, which can be enjoyed in comfortable surroundings while taking advantage of the panoramic views over the first lagoon.

Other information:
- Car park and toilets
- Entrance to the Nature Reserve is free for RSPB Members, small charge for non-members – refundable against taking out membership subscription
- Opening hours 10 a.m. – 5 p.m., every day except Christmas Day, Waterside Coffee Shop 10 a.m. – 4 p.m.

What other sights are nearby:
- Historic walled town of Conwy and castle
- Victorian seaside resort of Llandudno
- Great Orme's Head
- Little Orme's Head
- Caerhun church and Tal-y-cafn bridge
- National Trust Bodnant Garden

Originally published in
Birds, Boots and Butties: Conwy Valley/Eastern Snowdonia
by Ruth Miller

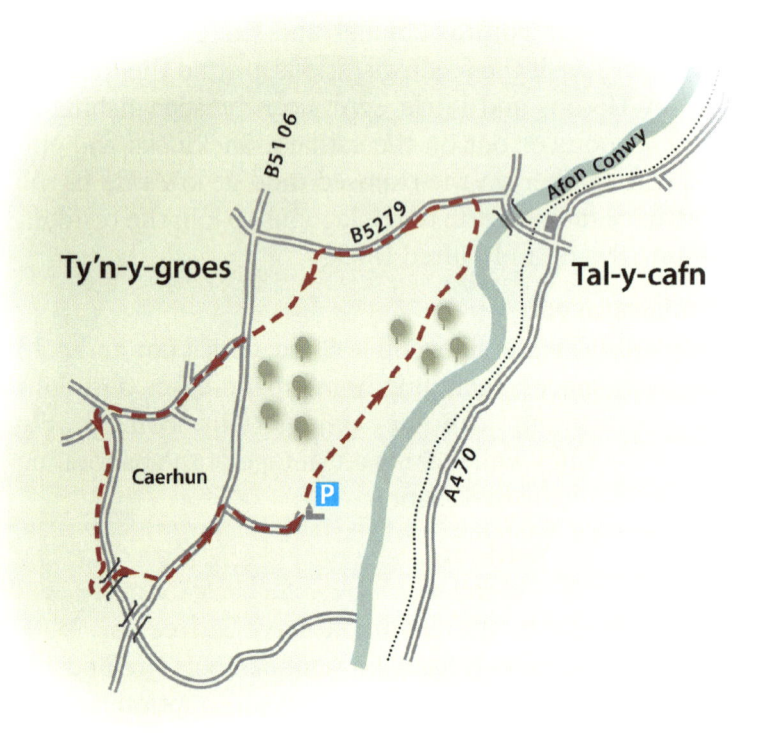

Walk 9
Caerhun church and the Conwy valley

Walk details

Approx distance: *3 miles/4.8 kilometres*
(Circular walk: 4½ miles/7.2 kilometres)

Approx time: *1-1½ hours there and back*
2 hours – circular walk

O.S. Maps: *1:50 000 Landranger Sheet 115*
1:20 000 Explorer OL 17

Start: *Grid Ref. SH 776 704*

Access: *From Conwy town, take the B5106 south towards Betws-y-coed for about 5 miles/8 km. Approximately 1 mile/1.6 km after the crossroads with the B5279 in Ty'n-y-groes, you reach the hamlet of Caerhun. Turn left down a single track road, signposted '13th Century Church'. Continue to the end of this lane.*

Parking: *Park in the small area beside the churchyard, taking care not to block farm gateways.*

Please note: *Due to church services, parking is not allowed here on Sunday mornings. If you visit at this time, continue on the B5106 for a few hundred metres beyond the lane, where there is a larger lay-by slightly further down the hill on the left-hand side of the B-road.*

Going: *Easy walking on footpaths and country lanes.*

Caerhun church

Site highlights
- Historic church and site of Roman fort of Canovium.
- Views of Conwy valley, and the hills of Tal y Fan and Pen y Gaer.
- Waders on Afon Conwy seen from Caerhun churchyard and Tal-y-cafn bridge.

Headline description
This gentle walk is set in the attractive Conwy valley. It starts in the peaceful setting of Caerhun churchyard, which gives good views over stretches of Afon Conwy which are otherwise unreachable, an ideal spot for winter birding. The 13th century church is built on the site of Canovium Roman Fort, an auxiliary fort between Chester and Caernarfon. There are also signs of a civilian settlement, including a bathhouse by the river itself, and part of the walk follows the route of the original Roman track. The Tal-y-cafn bridge allows good views of birds on the mudflats exposed at low

tide on Afon Conwy. On the return leg, you are rewarded with a clear view of the beautiful Tal y Fan and Pen y Castell hills, which lie within the Eryri/Snowdonia National Park.

Walk directions
Start by walking into the churchyard for views overlooking Afon Conwy.

Ancient yew trees, contemporary with the 13th century church, stationed around the churchyard, are often alive with birds; keep a sharp eye open for the elusive Hawfinch in winter in particular. In early spring, snowdrops carpet the ground.

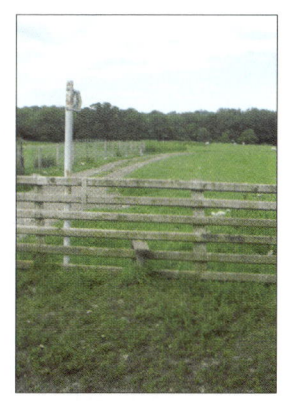

Returning to the parking area, climb the stile to your right and follow the track downhill towards the river. Go through the gate into the next field, still following the track. 150m before you reach the cottage at the riverside, leave the track and bear left to the ladder stile in the left-hand corner of the field. Walk straight across the next field towards the trees and cross the stile into the woodland.

Beech woodland is uncommon in this part of the country so it is worth taking the time to look for woodland birds. Beech trees are also the favoured habitat for Hawfinches, so look carefully for this elusive bird. You are very likely to see Pheasants as they are encouraged around here, though not if you choose the shooting season for your walk when they're likely to be lying low!

Follow the path straight through this narrow strip of mainly beech woodland and over the next stile into the field. Follow the right-hand edge of this field, with good views of Tal-y-Fan to your left. Pass through the gate and cross the farmyard, following the track round to the left of the large barn signalled by the yellow-top footpath sign. Continue round behind the barn and follow the track with the farmhouse on your right and farmsteading on your left. The track continues downhill and is closer to the river here.

The damp shady conditions here are ideal for Marsh Marigolds, and in spring their bright yellow flowers combine with daffodils to make this a very pretty stretch.

Follow the track until you reach some houses and the B5279. Turn right and cross the Tal-y-cafn Bridge, looking up – and downstream for waders as you do so.

This stretch of the river is tidal, and at low tide, significant areas of mud are exposed, attracting a variety of waders, gulls and the occasional Goosander. Common Sandpipers are usually regular visitors here in the summer months, while you may also see Sand Martins by the inner bank of the river where it curves left, upstream from the bridge.

Continue over the level crossing and the Tal-y-cafn pub, which serves refreshments, is on your left by the T-junction. For a short there-and-back walk, go back up the B5279 and retrace your steps along the track back to Caerhun church.

For a slightly longer walk, continue along the B-road as it goes uphill and then narrows. Just before reaching the houses of Ty'n-y-groes, take the footpath on the left to cut off the corner. Go through the kissing gate marked by the footpath sign into the field, and bear right round to the next stile. Cross this next field, keeping to the left-hand side of the field edge.

In summer, this is a stunning area for wild flowers and butterflies, including Tortoiseshells, Red Admirals and Peacocks.

Climb the stile out onto the B5106. From here, it is a short walk back along the road to Caerhun.

For those wishing to walk further, cross over the B road and follow the country lane on the right-hand side of the house towards Ro-wen. Follow along this to the end of the lane.

In summer, check the hedgerows and telephone wires as you go for Greenfinches and Goldfinches. Spotted Flycatchers have been seen here. Blackberries and hazelnuts occur along here in autumn.

Turn right and enjoy the views down the Conwy valley as you walk down the lane

towards the hamlet of Pontwgan. Turn left here over the road bridge crossing Afon Ro. Pass Mill Cottage and climb the stile on your left, marked by the footpath sign, into the field. Keeping with the hedge on to your left drop down to the next stile beside the trees and cross into the water meadow by the river, enjoying the seats thoughtfully provided here. Cross the next four stiles keeping the river on your left.

Keep your eyes peeled for Dippers and Grey Wagtails on this clear, rocky little stream. Himalyan Balsam, an attractive though unfortunately pervasive invader, has also reached even this secluded stretch of water.

When you reach the fifth stile and the farm lane, turn left to where it joins the B5106. Turn left, walk up past the cemetery and turn right into the lane leading back to Caerhun church.

Just before you reach the church, where two oak trees straddle the lane, you can quite clearly see the embankment demarcating the area of the Roman Fort of Canovium.

What to look for ...
... in spring/summer: You are likely to hear and see warblers such as Willow Warblers, Chiffchaffs and Blackcaps in the willows along Afon Ro and beside Afon Conwy, while you may be lucky and see Spotted Flycatchers along your walk.

... in autumn: Look out for Redwings and Fieldfares passing through, particularly around any berried trees.

... in winter: Caerhun churchyard is one of the regular sites in northern Wales to see Hawfinches in winter. Check the tall trees along the road to the church, and

Afon Conwy near Caerhun

pines from outside the churchyard. They may also be seen in the stretch of woodland you walk through, where they may be attracted by the beech trees. From the churchyard, you can look down onto Afon Conwy where gulls and geese collect on the shallows and banks. Look out for Herring, Common and Black-headed Gulls, and you may be lucky enough to see a Mediterranean Gull. Greylag and Canada Geese gather here. You may see Wigeon, Teal and Goldeneye on the river here, and nearer Tal-y-cafn bridge. Dippers can often be seen on Afon Ro.

... all year round: The churchyard is a great place to see Goldfinches, Greenfinches and Chaffinches in good numbers. Goldcrests also occur in the ancient yew trees here. You will frequently trip over both male and female Pheasants in the beech wood and you may hear and see Jays too. Down on the river, you should see Mute Swans, Mallards, and Red-breasted

Hawfinch

Mergansers and Goosanders, and Common Sandpipers have been regularly seen by the Tal-y-cafn Bridge. Grey Wagtails can be seen on the small rushing Afon Ro all year. Keep an eye open for rarities that can occur at any time here. Sharp eyes have seen not only Otters but also a White Stork on Afon Conwy by Tal-y-cafn bridge!

Where to eat

At the time of writing, the café and shop at Tal-y-cafn were closed until further notice. The Groes Inn between Ty'n-y-groes and Conwy offers high standard inn food. Alternative refreshments can be found in the tearoom at the National Trust Bodnant Gardens, 10 minutes' drive away from Caerhun church. Return in your car along the B5106 towards Conwy. Turn right at Ty'n-y-groes onto the B5279 to Tal-y-cafn. At the main road, by the Tal-y-cafn pub, turn left onto the A470 towards Colwyn Bay. After ½ mile/0.8 km, turn right where signposted at the top of the hill for the National Trust Bodnant Gardens. The tearoom is open seven days a week from 10 a.m. to 5 p.m. from March to October, and 10 a.m. to 4 p.m. in the first half of November. It is closed the rest of the year.

Other information

- Parking by Caerhun church and nearby lay-bys. Large car park at Tal-y-cafn Hotel.
- Toilets at Tal-y-cafn Hotel for customers only.

Afon Conwy and Tal-y-cafn bridge

What other sights are nearby?
- Historic walled town of Conwy and castle.
- Conwy RSPB Reserve.
- Village of Betws-y-coed and the Gwydir Forest.
- National Trust Bodnant Gardens.
- Bodnant Food Centre.
- The nearby Groes Inn claims to be the oldest pub in Wales.

Originally published in
Birds, Boots and Butties: Conwy Valley/Eastern Snowdonia

by Ruth Miller

Carreg Gwalch Best Valley Walks in Snowdonia

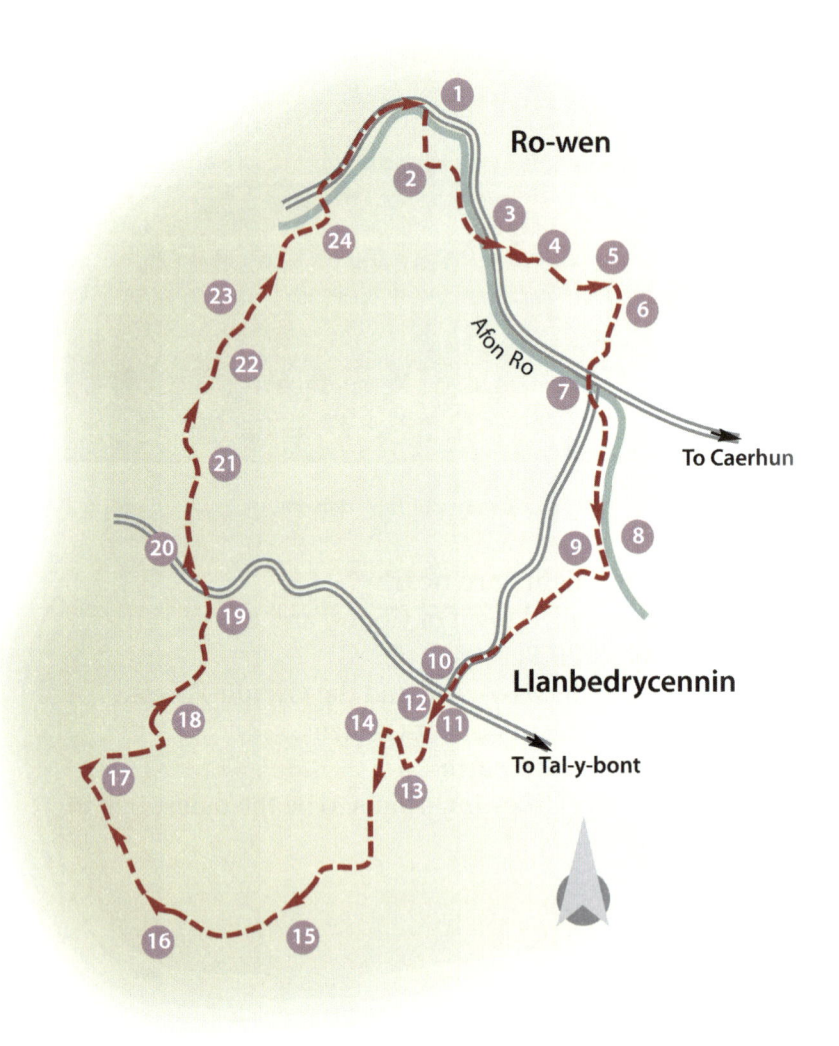

Ro-wen

Afon Ro

To Caerhun

Llanbedrycennin

To Tal-y-bont

Walk 10
Around Llanbedrycennin and Ro-wen

Walk details

Approx distance: 7 miles/11.3 *kilometres*

Approx time: 2½-3 hours

O.S. Maps: 1:50 000 *Landranger Sheet 115*
                    1:25 000 *Explorer OL 17*

Start: *Tŷ Gwyn Hotel, Ro-wen*
                    Grid Ref. SH 759 719

Access: *B5106 Conwy-Ro-wen. From the Groes Inn turn right for Ro-wen – you will reach your destination within 2 miles.*

Parking: *On the roadside in the middle of the village. Quiet road with plenty of parking spaces.*
                    Park at Ro-wen in layby on left beside footbridge or on the wide road between the Post Office and the Tŷ Gwyn Hotel 759719.
                    For those wishing to reach Pen y Gaer sooner there is limited parking in Llanbedrycennin a little east of Ye Olde Bull.

Please note: *Fields can be muddy during winter time.*
                    Between points 4 and 5 the fields are steep.
                    Rough walk at point 12, Bryn y Coed.
                    A lot of undergrowth on the way to Pen-y-gaer.

Going: *Quiet country lanes, fields and hill sides.*

The walk can be started from Ro-wen following the pleasant Afon Ro for a time, apart from a detour (optional) to climb a small hill for good views of the

Pen y Gaer from Bwlch y Ddeufaen

Conwy valley. After going through the attractive village of Llanbedrycennin, with its simple medieval church, old tracks take you fairly gently up into the hills for a visit to Pen y Gaer. This Iron Age fort has 3 ramparts. Below its main entrance in the south west you will find many pointed stones set in the ground. These 'cheveux de frise' slowed enemy charges down so that defenders had more time to launch their missiles (arrows and stones). The return goes gently down the open hillside back to the quiet village of Ro-wen. There are good views of the valley in the higher sections of the walk, also the Carneddau range of mountains are seen from an unusual angle. Paths are usually mostly dry except at Point 14. You can shorten the walk to 3¾

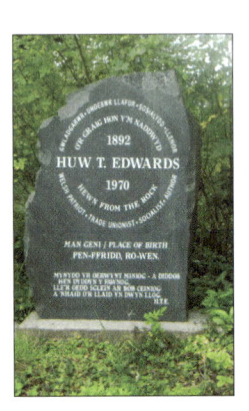

Memorial plaque at the start of the walk

miles/6km at Point 19 by forking right at lane junction.

Walk directions

1. Cross footbridge and go on, soon between walls.

2. Just before gate, turn left along by hedge, then right to walk by river (on your left).

3. Unless you wish to stay on the road to Point 7, turn left over road and right down steps. Go on over field towards farmhouse to a gate just left of house.

Kissing gate at Point 3 of the walk

4. On along grass, left before white gate, then through right gate past sheds. On 15m then go left up field with wall on right and poles.

5. At field corner cross the low but rather awkward fence and go

After farmhouse, path descends to left at Point 4 of the walk

The derelict farm at Pontwgan. The path goes between the farmhouse and the farm buildings, then out onto the road.

up field towards house. Then bear right to walk by iron fence. At hedge to left and at once right over stiles.

6. Go one third right to steps in hedge on crest of ridge. Go on down with hedge on your left. At next hedge go through the right-hand of 2 gaps and follow hedge (on your left) down to barn. Go on through gate just right of barn to road.

7. Go on across road, over bridge, and past houses to iron steps. Here go left to walk by Afon Ro.

8. Just after bridge on left go over stile. Cross field keeping near farm on right.

After crossing over a stone bridge, look out for this iron stile on your right, which leads down to a river; Point 7 of the walk

Llanbedrycennin church

9. Over stile near house and left to gate. Keep on with hedge on your right.

10. On along track, then road, past church to Ye Olde Bull.

11. Here fork right up lane and soon fork left.

12. At Bryn y Coed fork right up rough track. Go right through farm gate by pole and left along faint field path. Bear right by hedge (on your right) up to barns.

13. Here go left between barns and right along grass track passing just left of house

14. At next barns turn left up stony track. (If muddy go through gate on right beside pens and follow faint path in bracken parallel to track.).

Ye Olde Bull – a drovers' inn at Llanbedrycennin

15. When wall on left ends follow wall on right to leat. Go on by leat.

16. Turn right over first bridge and on along track.

17. Go right up ladder stile over wall. The fort is reached after crossing wall at a second stile. Return to this stile but turn right along wall without crossing it.

18. Soon a wall stile is reached. Here turn two-thirds right down the left of two banks. Keep on when bank ends to reach gate into lane.

19. Down lane. Fork left at lane junction.

20. As lane bears left cross stile over wall and go north over field to pass just left of large pylon. Here a grassy track leads to house. Use gate just right of house to reach road.

21. Turn left along road for 100m, then right between walls. Keep on over field with wall on your right. When wall bears right keep along clear path. When path becomes narrow make for ladder stile over wall about 100m ahead.

22. Over stile and on, soon beside sunken lane on right.

23. Over iron steps and down by fence and lane on right. Join track at gate.

24. Go over stile on right before house. Go down past sheep pens. Follow hedge for 50m and over stile on left. Go straight on past house on left to green gate, then straight on to road and right down it. Ignore turnings off to left.

Tŷ Gwyn inn, Ro-wen

Originally published in
Walks in North Snowdonia

by Don Hinson

Carreg Gwalch Best Valley Walks in Snowdonia

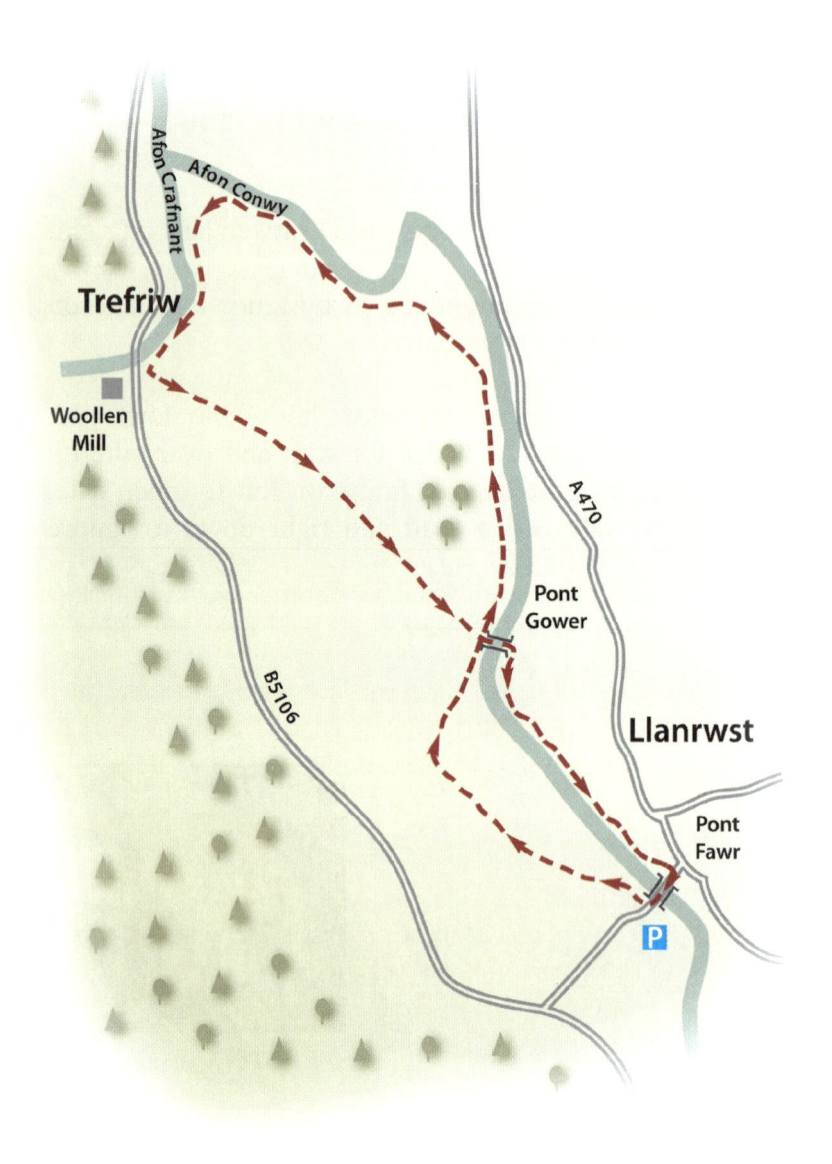

Walk 11
Tu Hwnt i'r Bont, Llanrwst

Walk details

Approx distance: *4 miles/6.4 kilometres*

Approx time: *1¾ hours (without including a stop at Trefriw)*

O.S. Maps: *1:50 000 Landranger Sheet 115*
1:25 000 Explorer OL 17

Start: *The old bridge, Llanrwst*
Grid Ref. SH 798 615

Access: *Cross the bridge from Llanrwst.*
Parking on your left.

Parking: *There is a free car park on the left after crossing the bridge from Llanrwst.*

Please note: *Riverside walk at Llanrwst can be dangerous when the river is high.*

Going: *Valley floor, on the level.*

This National Trust owned property, shrouded by virginia creeper, is a former courthouse where Sir John Wynn of nearby Gwydir sat in judgement over the people of Llanrwst. It is now a cafe serving teas, coffees and excellent scones.

The walk – from the old bridge at Llanrwst to Tu Hwnt i'r

Bont and then following the path along Afon Conwy to Trefriw and back to Llanrwst.

Start near the old bridge at Llanrwst – Pont Fawr. Cross the road towards Tu Hwnt i'r Bont, and then look for a Public Footpath sign on the right. Go down the track and after ½ km you will see a stile on your right just after a sharp bend to the left. Go over it and follow the path that runs along a ditch in the right-hand side of the field. Go over another stile and continue in the same direction past a small lake to another stile. Go over it and straight ahead over a small bridge and over a stile. You will then go over another stile and walk along the embankment that runs parallel to Afon Conwy.

Go to your right over the stile and continue along the embankment towards a bridge. An information board near the bridge explains recent steps taken to reduce flood risk in this area. Don't go over the footbridge (Pont Gower) nor to the left but go straight ahead over the two stiles and along the embankment. Go through the kissing gate and continue along the embankment and through another kissing gate near some pools. Continue along the embankment, through two kissing gates and then the path goes to the left away from the river.

Go through the kissing gate and continue along the embankment, then turn left and rejoin the river. Go through two kissing gates and continue along the

Looking back from Pont Gower

embankment before turning left towards Trefriw. Follow the embankment that now runs parallel to Afon Crafnant, through two kissing gates, but don't go over the bridge on your right. Go through the kissing gate to a track and a public footpath sign. Go through the gate and along the path that runs between two fences. Go through a gate, pass a public toilet on your left and go out into the main road at Trefriw. In front of you is the woollen mill. Why not spend some time in Trefriw? There are two pubs here, a cafe, shops and the chalybeate wells.

Turn left and follow the narrow road that goes past a caravan park (not the main road). At the end of the road, follow the path passing a flood lake on your right, over the new embankment, between the playing field and the recreation ground. You will then reach a lane; follow it for 1 km to the footbridge. Go over this and turn right, over the stile to the riverside path. Go over two stiles, keeping on the riverside path, until you come to the decking. Follow the decking causeway over the bridge, continuing on the slate path, passing St Grwst's church and then up the steps to the street. Turn right and go over the bridge back to the car park.

Looking back from Pont Gower

Tu Hwnt i'r Bont, Llanrwst

Other Points of Interest

Afon Conwy The river rises from Llyn Conwy near Penmachno in Snowdonia and over its 36-mile length drops nearly 1,500 feet before it reaches the coast near Conwy. Its short length makes its level rise and fall very quickly when it rains heavily in the mountains. The river is tidal up to Llanrwst (about 14 miles from the sea) and at one time small ships and boats used to sail as far as here. At the turn of the 20th century pleasure boats came up the river to Trefriw bringing trippers – up to a thousand a day – from Conwy, Llandudno and Deganwy, for fishing, climbing, painting and in the recreation ground golf, tennis, bowls, croquet and quoits. The chalybeate wells have attracted visitors here from the 1800s to take the sulphur-iron rich waters. The wells date back to the Roman period when the Twentieth Legion had its headquarters in Caerhun lower down the valley. During the 19th century the pump room and baths

Pont Gower

were developed as a curative centre. Trefriw's heyday as a tourist resort ended during the Second World War due to silting of the river, but visitors still come here by car and bus to visit the spa baths and woollen mill.

Embankment The cob was built around 1815 although there have been numerous extensions and improvements since then. The valley was prone to flooding a number of times a year and the ground tended to be waterlogged and difficult to farm. At the beginning of the 19th century, the Reverend Walter Davies described the land as '… a perfect bog, partly peat, partly clay, producing a scanty crop of short and sour hay.' The main landowner, the Earl of Ancaster, embarked on a scheme to improve the farmland by digging drainage ditches and enclosing the land with the embankment. Despite the defences, the Conwy broke through the embankment and flooded the area twice in 2004, after very heavy rain.

Pont Fawr, Llanrwst

Pont Gower The original bridge was a timber trestle construction built in the 19th century to link Trefriw with the railway station in Llanrwst, from where visitors would be taken by horse-drawn carriage to the Trefriw health spa. Some of the timber foundations of the original bridge are still visible underneath the modern suspension bridge.

Pont Fawr It is believed to have been designed by Inigo Jones and was built in 1636. This graceful triple-arched structure served the ancient counties of Caernarfonshire and Denbighshire as the only valley crossing until the construction of Thomas Telford's iron bridge at Betws-y-coed and suspension bridge at Conwy in the 19th century. Pont Fawr Llanrwst was a vital component in the defence of northern Wales during the English Civil War and in the latter half of the conflict Royalist troops blew up the western arch of the bridge to halt the advance of Parliamentarian artillery.

Llanrwst – is a town shrouded in myth, legend and a history dating back 1,500 years and having altered very little in the last 400 years. By the 10th century there was a sizeable settlement on this site, which in AD 954 saw the brutal and bloody Battle of Llanrwst, a decisive battle between the forces of northern and southern Wales. The town was wasted by an English army in 1403 because of its staunch support of Owain Glyndŵr's revolution and it suffered once again during the Wars of the Roses, when it was completely destroyed by Yorkist troops under the leadership of William Herbert, Earl of Pembroke. The town is proud of its independent roots and found itself in the No Man's Land of past wars. It still bears the motto: *'Cymru, Lloegr a Llanrwst'* (Wales, England and Llanrwst). Llanrwst Almshouses were constructed in 1610 by Sir John Wynn of Gwydir to house twelve poor men of the parish. They continued to provide shelter until 1976 when the buildings closed. Then in 1996 with the aid of Heritage Lottery funding they were restored and in 2002 opened as a museum of local history and a community focal point. It consists of two restored period rooms, temporary exhibitions and local artefacts. A working herb garden is situated in the museum grounds. Sadly the museum is closed at present

St Grwst's church It is dedicated to the Celtic saint Grwst, a 6th century Welsh missionary who settled in Dyffryn Conwy. The present church, although constructed in 1170, dates from 1470, rebuilt two years

St Grwst church, Llanrwst

after its destruction by Yorkist troops. The church houses a beautiful rood screen, a relic of the Cistercian Abbey at Maenan, built in 1509. The Wynn side-chapel was built in 1634 as a family mausoleum and houses rare examples of Stuart-period memorials. The chapel is home to the stone sarcophagus of Llywelyn ap Iorwerth, known as Llywelyn Fawr, and the effigy of Hywel Coetmor, a local knight who fought under the Black Prince at Poitiers and returned home to participate in the Glyndŵr Rebellion. Both structures are Grade I listed buildings. Open for accompanied viewing are a reproduction of a fresco depicting the Last Supper (from the Santa Maria Monastery in Milan), the ancient Llanrwst Bell and the spur of Dafydd ap Siencyn, the local 15th century outlaw. The church has recently undergone a programme of restoration funded by the Heritage Lottery Fund.

The woollen mill at Trefriw

Trefriw At one time Trefriw was an important trading centre and was regarded as the biggest inland port in Wales. Merchandise was brought up river from the coast and boats returned with slate, ore and timber from the surrounding hills. It was also an important wool-manufacturing centre. The mill was established before the industrial revolution, with its fulling mill taking already woven cloth from the cottages to wash and finish.

Originally published in
National Trust Walks 1. Northern Wales

by Dafydd Meirion

Carreg Gwalch Best Valley Walks in Snowdonia

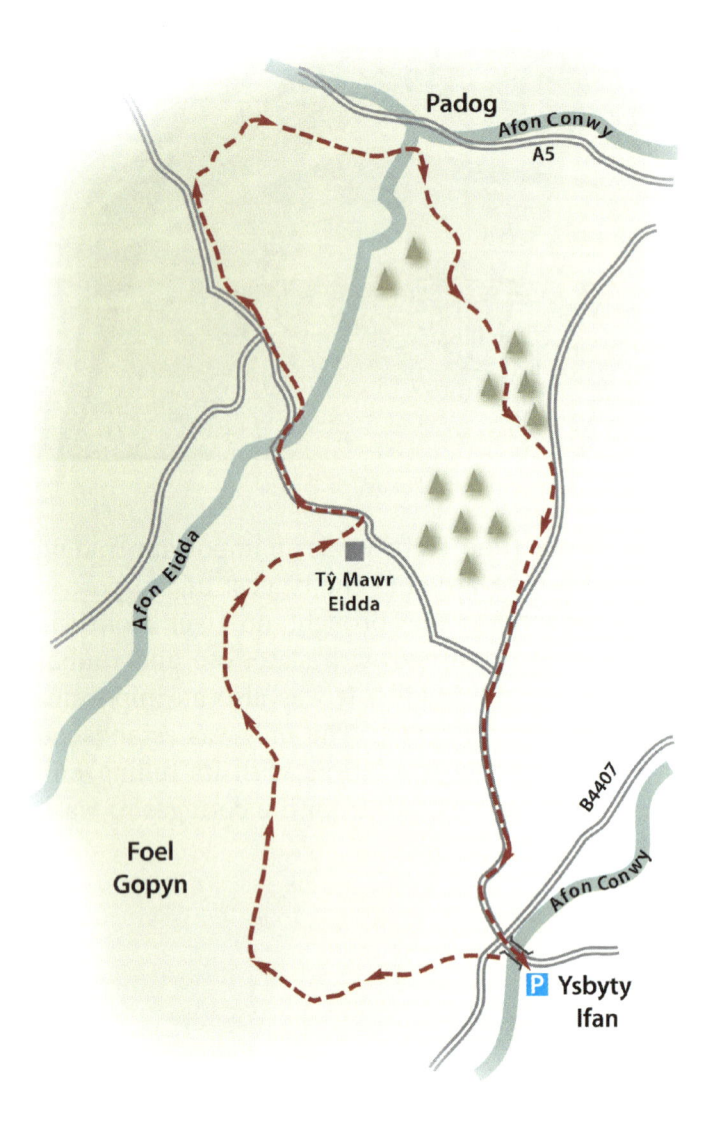

Walk 12
Ysbyty Ifan, upper Conwy valley

Walk details
Approx distance: *5½ miles/8.8 kilometres*

Approx time: *3 hours*

O.S. Maps: *1:50 000 Landranger Sheet 116*
1:25 000 Explorer OL 18

Start: *By the bridge, Ysbyty Ifan*
Grid Ref. SH 843 488

Access: *There is an infrequent bus service to Ysbyty Ifan. You should ring Traveline Cymru (0870 6082608) if you intend travelling there by bus.*

Parking: *There is space for about half a dozen cars to park near the old mill at Ysbyty Ifan. Turn left out of the mill and then right at the next turning past the old almshouses (see plaque on the gable end).*

Please note: *Traditional farmland – please abide by usual code.*

Going: *Country paths and lanes.*

In 1856, Lord Penrhyn, owner of the Penrhyn quarries who lived at Penrhyn Castle, bought the Ysbyty Estate which had over thirty farms, from the then owners Sir Edward Pryce Lloyd and Edward Mostyn Lloyd. The estate provided substantial rents for Lord Penrhyn as records show. For example, the widow of a Robert Hughes who rented the mill and the meadow in 1870 paid a rent of £27.10.00 per year. The rent collected from the whole village – a total of about a hundred

The bridge over Afon Conwy, Ysbyty Ifan

farms and homes – was £1,703.13.00, which was a considerable sum for those days.

The National Trust owns and manages the 52 farms which are on the estate today, as well as the old mill.

There is space for about half a dozen cars to park near the old mill at Ysbyty Ifan and a few parking spaces over the other side of the bridge. There is an infrequent bus service to Ysbyty Ifan. You should ring Traveline Cymru (0870 6082608) if you intend travelling there by bus. Turn left out of the mill and then right at the next turning past the old almshouses (see plaque on the gable end).

Go up the hill; don't turn right into the farm but keep straight up along the rough track to a gate. Go through it and proceed along the track to another gate. Go through it and up the track to a lane. Turn right and go along the lane to the crest of the hill and then down, keeping to the lane.

Ignore the lane on the left going to Foel Gopyn and

the footpath sign on the right and go straight ahead along the road. Turn right by a gate, follow the track ignoring the stile on your right. Go through the gate next to the cattle grid and follow the lane down the hill. You will come to a farm called Pen-y-bryn, don't enter the farm, follow the lane to the right.

Go through the gate and along the lane to another gate and through the farmyard of Tŷ Nant and then right through a gate, up the lane and to the left, over a bridge and through two gates. Ignore the turning to the right and continue down the hill. Also ignore the stile near the cowshed and go right and up the hill towards Tŷ Mawr. Go through two gates through the farmyard until you come to another lane.

Turn left and down the hill and over the bridge that crosses Afon Eidda. Ignore the stile on the left and go up the hill keeping to the lane, ignoring a lane to the left and right and the lane to Fron Ddu. Then go through the gate towards Bryn Bras on your right. Go along the lane, through a gate, through the farmyard and to the right and along the track through two gates. Cross the stream and down to a gate. Don't go through this gate but go left along the fence to a small gate. Go through it, along the path through the trees with the river on your right, over the footbridge and out near the A5 close to a telephone kiosk at Padog.

Go to the right to a large expanse of tarmac. To the right

is Capel Padog. Follow the path between the garage and the house to a gate. Go through it and up along the wall to a kissing gate and then straight up aiming for two trees and an old wall and a footpath sign. Continue up the slope until you see a farm ahead, aim for a farm. When you reach the fence go to the left and you will reach a stile. Go over it and go to the right towards the farm. You will then reach a footpath sign and a kissing gate.

Go up the field with a forest on your left and to a kissing gate. Go through it and when you have gone past the trees you will see a kissing gate on your left. Go through it and over a small wooden bridge and to a track up ahead. Go right to the top of the hill through a gate and to a junction. Keep straight ahead to the top of the hill and through a gate and to another gate and junction. Go straight ahead and down the hill and back to Ysbyty Ifan.

Other Points of Interest

A5 Built by Thomas Telford, after pressure to improve the mail service between London and Dublin, work started on this route in 1815. Up until the 1990s it was the main route into northern Wales, connecting with the ferry service to Ireland in Holyhead. The road starts from the Marble Arch in London and then follows the old Roman road (Watling Street) to the Welsh border, marked by a bridge over the river Dee. After winding its way

The old mill, Ysbyty Ifan

through Snowdonia, it crosses the Menai Strait and proceeds along Anglesey to the ferry terminal at Holyhead. The A5 has now been given the status of a Historic Route.

Popty Pen Uchaf The bakery is a venture by one of the tenants of the National Trust's upland farms. Only the best ingredients are used in the traditional recipes and the products are on sale in local shops.

The Old Mill The mill, which was built around 1800, served the neighbouring farms and was an integral part of the village. It is likely that the mill was established on the recommendation of Lord Penrhyn who had the legal right to insist that all the corn grown by his tenants should be ground in his mill. The influence of local mills such as this one in Ysbyty Ifan declined in the early twentieth century with the growth of larger companies in urban areas. By 1940, the last miller,

The church at Ysbyty Ifan

Thomas John Roberts, had started supplementing his income by using the mill to generate electricity for the village. But it was not sufficient for the needs of all the village, and the further from the mill the lower the power. The mill closed around 1960 and in 1997 it became a listed building. The old water-wheel is still behind the mill as well as some of the old machinery inside.

Pen y Bont The village Post Office and Gwniadur are situated in part of the farmhouse. Gwniadur offers a dressmaking, millinery and wedding finery service.

Ysbyty Ifan The original name of the village was Dolgynwal, but it changed when a hospice and garrison was established here in 1190. The *ysbyty* or hospice was established by Hospice Knights, later better known as the Knights of St John of Jerusalem. It became a refuge for travellers and received support from wealthy local landowners and the village grew around it as well as becoming a rich agricultural area. There is a plaque on the present church which is on the site of the old hospice. The knights were given certain exemptions and immunities from the law, so that no officer of the crown could enter their property to arrest lawbreakers. It is said that the immunity was never repealed and the hospice became a refuge for bandits who terrorised the neighbourhood at the end of the Middle Ages.

Originally published in
National Trust Walks 1. Northern Wales

by Dafydd Meirion

Carreg Gwalch Best Valley Walks in Snowdonia

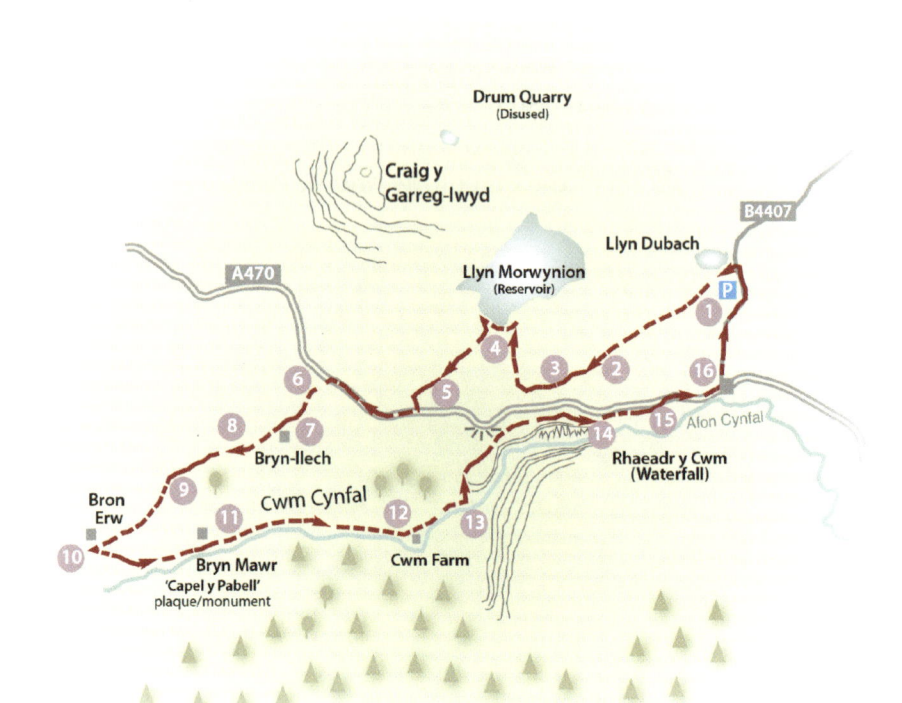

Walk 13
Cwm Cynfal, Ffestiniog

Walk details

Approx distance: 4½ miles/7 kilometres

Approx time: *3 hours*

O.S. Maps: 1:50 000 *Landranger Sheet 124*
1:25 000 *Explorer OL 18*

Start: *Llyn Dubach*
Grid Ref. SH 746 424

Access: *Off B4407, north of junction with B4391 at Pont yr Afon Gam*

Parking: *Park by the southern edge of Llyn Dubach by the B4407, ¼ mile (0.5 km) north of the junction with the B4391, 3 miles (5 km) east from Ffestiniog. Or park by Pont Newydd on A470 (714 409) and walk north-east along minor road to join walk at point 10.*

Going: *Paths are usually good, but one patch could be wet in stage 14.*

Summary

After glimpses of Llyn Morynion (*'Lake of the Maidens'*) a broad ridge is descended with good views including the Moelwyn mountains. The return starts in the attractive valley beside Afon Cynfal. The climax is reached as the path climbs out of the spectacular cwm with its fine waterfall – Rhaeadr-y-cwm.

Llyn Morynion

Walk directions

1. From car park, go along track which bears L to a gate. Go through and on at 45° to fence over grass. (To see more of the lake when it comes into view, bear R over grass dodging marshy areas to join edge path.)
2. Pass just R of marshy area, now along grass track towards line of poles.
3. Go on under poles to join clear stony track by wall on its L. It bears R then (near lake) L.
4. Take L fork towards road, with wall near your L.
5. Turn R down road.
6. After going down towards bend sign, turn L along clear track.
7. When track turns L keep straight on along grass path. Through wall gap and on with wall on your R.
8. Cross low fence, now with fence and wall on your R. After 100m at fence gap go half L down field to wall gap beside ruin.
9. Keep on beside old sunken track. The track is later

raised up. Join it and carry on through farm to road.
10. Turn L along road.
11. Ignore track forking R down to bridge.
12. At Cwm Farm keep on along field edge with wall on your R.
13. Over ladder stile and L up steep path.
14. At a marshy patch path bears R, soon with old wall or fence on the R. (If wet, detour to the L.) At top, cross fence for precipitous view down ravine.
15. As path becomes vague bear L to walk near road and join road at gate.
16. Turn L at road junction.

The upper part of Cwm Cynfal

Other paths near this walk
Paths just N and W of Llyn Morynion seem to have gone, and the path NW from the road at 743 419 is reedy and hard to follow.

Originally published in *Walks in North Snowdonia* by Don Hinson

Cnicht

Llynnau Diffwys

Rhosydd Quarry

Llyn Croesor

Croesor Quarry

Afon Croesor

Cwm Croesor

Croesor

Walk 14
Cwm Croesor

Walk details

Approx distance: 5½ miles/9 kilometres

Approx time: 4 hours

O.S. Maps: 1:50 000 *Landranger Sheet 124*
1:25 000 *Explorer OL 18*

Start: *Croesor car park*
Grid Ref. SH 631 447

Access: *From A4085 at Garreg, Llanfrothen, follow narrow lane north-eastwards signposted Croesor*

Parking: *Croesor car park*

Please note: *Don't attempt the walk in mist.*
Choose a dry season or a different walk if you don't like marshy ground.

Going: *Paths are generally good except for 400m of pathless progress between Rhosydd Quarry and Llynnau Diffwys, where one or two marshy areas can cause problems.*

Summary

This walk takes you gently up the valley side to the fascinating ruins of Croesor and Rhosydd Quarries, then across the valley top to remote lakes before a splendid little-known path goes back on the other side. There is much beauty to be seen, and the limited scars that mining operations have left help you to imagine the past scene without spoiling the general outlook.

Cwm Croesor

Walk directions
1. Turn L out of the car park and soon L along the valley road.
2. At house go ½R up track.
3. At quarry gates, go over stile and on 50m. Here take the path just behind the ruin on your R. This slants up the hill to a point directly above and beyond the far ruin (the end of a roofless building).
4. Down over the L end of Llyn Croesor and on to Rhosydd Quarry. (May be wettish near the end.)
5. Cross the slaty flat area to find a cairn 70m L of falls. Follow the slight path up.
6. Fork L at an outcrop on your R, to walk along a mini-ridge and reach a line of posts in a marshy area. Here turn ⅓R up dry grass, passing two perched blocks. Keep on to the top, thus crossing a small marsh and steeply rising to a larger marsh that can be avoided on the R.
7. Turn L to get round the L of the two lakes seen.

Cnicht above Cwm Croesor

Follow small path that runs in marshy ground for 150m near the lake edge and crosses a stream. Then go gently up (E) small rise and on down.

8. When lake is seen, bear L to cross its dam. Follow large pipe (kept on your R) down.
9. Leave pipe when clear path is reached.
10. At ruin go ½L to bridge and on to join track.
11. Go L along road.

Originally published in
New Walks in Snowdonia

by Don Hinson

Carreg Gwalch Best Valley Walks in Snowdonia

Walk 15
Afon Tryweryn

Walk details

Approx distance: 3½ miles/5.5 kilometres

Approx time: 2½ hours

O.S. Maps: 1:50 000 *Landranger* Sheet 125
1:25 000 *Explorer* OL 18

Start: *Grid Ref. SH 913 385*

Access: *Off the A4214 (Trawsfynydd/Y Bala)*

Parking: *220m north of the point where the A4212 crosses Afon Tryweryn, ¾ mile (1 km) south of the B4501 junction. Here (Grid Ref. SH 913 385) park off the road where a track runs nearly parallel to the road.*

Going: *Parts of the walk go over fields without paths, but route finding is qute easy*

Summary

After passing through the reservoir of Llyn Celyn – which is still a raw wound in the history of drowning Welsh valleys – Afon Tryweryn bears S towards Bala. One of the few stretches of riverside path makes up the start of this walk. Then there is a climb over largely open rural country with fine views down to Llyn Tegid (Bala Lake) and the high mountains beyond, with the long stretch of the Aran range nearest.

Celyn memorial chapel on the shore of the reservoir

Walk directions

1. Go through gate and along the surfaced track nearly parallel to road. Keep on at its end, soon by river. 
2. On into wood, Path rises, then sharply drops to next stile. Then it climbs again, later by a line of stones on your L.
3. At wire fence, cross it where the barbs have been removed. Cross field to distant gate. 
4. Here go on along track.
5. Turn R along lane.
6. Turn L along farm drive for 60m, then on through gate and along grass track.
7. Well past the farm a gate is reached. Here go up ½L up field, passing L of cottage and on to field corner.

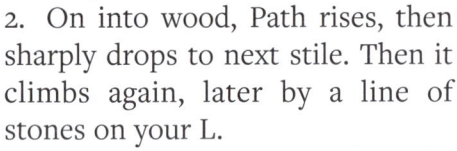

8. Here turn L along lane.

9. Where lane turns L, go R along track. Soon fork L through gate and go to L of first buildings. Turn L through gate 20m before reaching barn on your L. Walk along the R side of a line of small trees.

10. Cross fence 20m R of trees, where some stones make this easier. On over field to buildings. A track is joined.

11. On past first building (kept on your R) and second (on L). Go through gate and ½L to go through next gate and down track with fence on your L. Soon L through gate and over field to end of fence on your R.

12. Here sharp R through gate and down field near trees (and stream) on the R. Soon track is joined.

13. Turn L along lane.

14. At footpath sign, turn R down field with fence on your R.

15. Go R over stile and L with fence on your L.

16. Go ½L over field to gate by farm. Through gate and L by fence. Through next gate and R along track.

An easier walk, saving 1.5 km (1 mile)

Follow stages 1 to 4, then turn L along lane. (Once the wood is passed, views are good.)

14. At footpath sign, turn L down field with fence on your R. Follow stage 15 and on.

Originally published in
New Walks in Snowdonia
by Don Hinson

Carreg Gwalch Best Valley Walks in Snowdonia

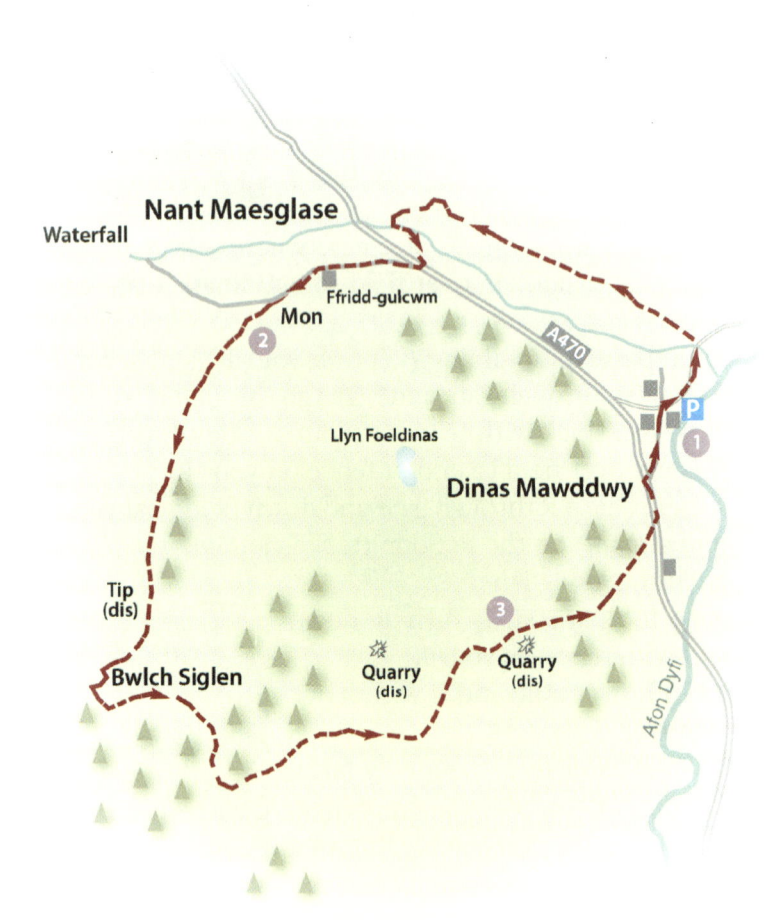

Walk 16
Nant Maesglase, Dinas Mawddwy

Walk details

Approx distance: 5¾ miles/9.3 kilometres

Approx time: 3½-4 hours

O.S. Maps: 1:50 000 *Landranger Sheet 124*
                   1:25 000 *Explorer OL 23*

Start: *Road junction at the Red Lion in Dinas Mawddwy Grid Ref. SH 858 148*

Access: *Dinas Mawddwy is just off the A470, 16km east of Dolgellau. Infrequent buses from Dolgellau*

Parking: *Y Plas – about 100 metres from the Red Lion*

Going: *Moderate – tracks, forest and hill paths*

Points of Interest:

1. Dinas Mawddwy was the territory of Gwylliaid Cochion Mawddwy (*'the Red Bandits of Mawddwy'*). On his tour in the 18th century, Thomas Pennant was told that travellers preferred to cross mountain summits on their way to England, rather than take the road. Scythes were placed in chimneys to prevent the bandits entering houses by the rooftops. In 1554, eighty bandits were executed, but the surviving outlaws killed the sheriff responsible for the deaths. They too were caught and executed. When Pennant visited Dinas Mawddwy he saw the stocks and whipping post, but was told that nobody had been whipped for several years. George Borrow, seventy years later, heard sounds of

drunken revelry from the huts, and saw fierce looking red haired men staggering about. Lead and slate mining used to be the main industries in the area.

2. The memorial is to Hugh Jones (1749-1825), a Calvinist Methodist hymn writer who lived in the lovely valley of the Nant Maesglase. Higher up the valley, the stream tumbles down Craig Maesglase as a spectacular waterfall. Lead and copper were worked in the Red Dragon mine, before attempts were made in 1854 to extract gold. Mining was unsuccessful and it closed in 1856.

3. Minllyn quarry employed over 100 men in its extensive open and underground workings. However,

The Hugh Jones memorial stone

it did not have a high output and closed around 1916. Remains include a chimney, a ruined mill and other buildings, and a tramway tunnel leading into a pit. The incline brought material from Cae Abaty quarry,

Minllyn quarry

located near the forest. Half a mile east of Minllyn lies a hill slope known as Maes Camlan. It is said to be the site of King Arthur's last battle, when he fought Mordred.

Walk Directions: **(-) denotes Point of Interest**

1. From the Red Lion (*Y Llew Coch*) in Dinas Mawddwy (1), take the road in the direction of Llanymawddwy. In 400 metres, cross a bridge and turn left on a track which leads into a caravan site.

2. Almost immediately take a track on the right. Go through a field above the site, and follow a fence. Pass through some trees and rhododendrons. Emerge from the trees and bear right on a path, uphill, towards conifers. Cross a broken gate, and turn left on a grassy track.

3. Keep ahead along the track, pass a house and continue on a

lane. Bear left at a fork, and cross a bridge. Reach a lane junction and turn left to the main road.

4. Turn right, and in 80 metres, turn left on a lane and follow it for 800 metres. As the lane descends to cross Nant Maesglase, and just before the land bends right, take a level track on the left at a footpath signpost.

5. Pass a monument (2) and go through a gate. Follow the green track along the hillside. Pass a plantation on the left, and cross a stile.

6. The path becomes rougher and crosses a stream. Pass the mine ruins, and continue on a path that slants uphill to the coniferous trees on the skyline.

7. The path becomes fainter just before it reaches the ridge. At Bwlch Siglen it meets another path in front of the forest. Turn left, and in a few paces, cross a stile into the forest.

8. Descend the path through the forest, and in about 120 metres reach a post with yellow arrows. Go left, following a broken wall at first.

9. Emerge on a forest track, and turn left. In a few paces, turn right on a track which narrows to a path. Pass a ruin on the right and look for yellow arrows. About 100 metres beyond the ruin, bear left at a fork in the path.

10. Stay on this path, and bear right with it to cross a stream and stile. Go sharp left, following the forest on your left. Reach some fencing and a stile, cross a stream and bear right, uphill, following the path parallel to the stream.

11. Towards the head of the valley, the path veers left (north), and reaches a plateau. Keep ahead, descending towards the tips of the disused Minllyn slate quarry. Before reaching the quarry, go down into a gully, keep to the right, and follow the incline towards the remains of buildings (3).

12. At the ruins, you will reach a corner fence with arrows. Follow the fence on the right, cross and bear left on a slaty path.

13. Descend with tips on your right, and emerge on another path. Bear right downhill, cross directly over a broad track to a path, and follow it to the A470.

14. Turn left, and shortly go right on a road leading to the Llew Coch in Dinas Mawddwy.

Facilities:
Public toilets near the start. Pub and camp site in Dinas Mawddwy. Meirion Woollen Mill.

Originally published in
Circular Walks in Meirionnydd

by Dorothy Hamilton

Carreg Gwalch Best Valley Walks in Snowdonia

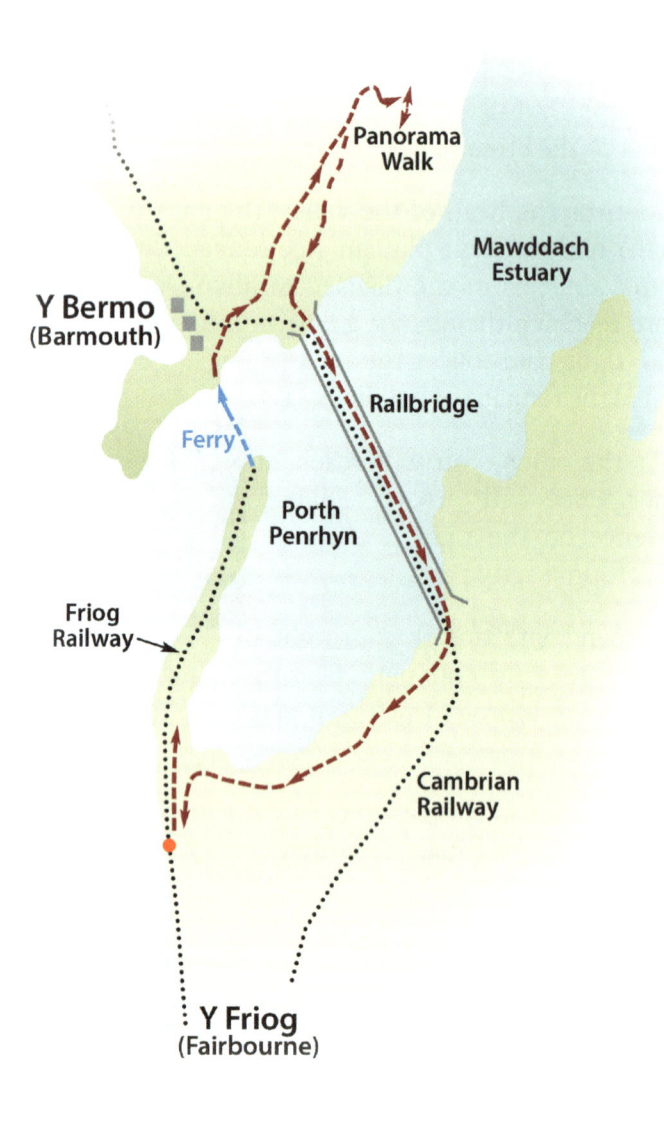

Panorama Walk

Mawddach Estuary

Y Bermo (Barmouth)

Railbridge

Ferry

Porth Penrhyn

Friog Railway

Cambrian Railway

Y Friog (Fairbourne)

Walk 17
Mawddach Estuary

Walk details

Approx distance: *4 miles/6.5 kilometres*

Approx time: *2½ hours*

O.S. Maps: *1:50 000 Landranger Sheet 124*
1:25 000 Explorer OL 23

Start: *On the seafront at Friog*
Grid Ref. SH 611 137

Parking: *Half way along the seafront at Friog* (Fairbourne)

Please note: *Ferry – April-Oct 11.00-5.30 (tide permitting)*
Railway – April-Oct (information 01341 250362)

Going: *Dunes to mountain paths*

Afon Mawddach has carved a great cleft into the coastline of Wales at its estuary, amidst spectacular mountain scenery. This walk, combined with a ride on a very narrow gauge railway and a ferry crossing, explores the estuary from both the sea and the mountainside. It starts at Friog (Fairbourne), a seaside resort with fine beaches and a railway, one of the Great Little Trains of Wales. A trip along the dunes by train or, if you prefer, on foot brings you to Porth Penrhyn Station. Here a passenger ferry is caught across the estuary to Y Bermo (*Barmouth*) quay.

The quay is central to Y Bermo's existence. A survey taken in 1565 showed that two small ferry boats were

Mawddach estuary from the southern hills

operating here even then. Rivers have always played a vital role in our trade and communications and so an estuary, where goods travelling on inland waterways can continue their journey upon the open sea, is doubly important. It is therefore no surprise that Afon Mawddach had its shipbuilding yards long ago and that between 1750 and 1865, three hundred and eighteen vessels were launched here.

The bulk of this early trade out of Y Bermo was timber from the local forests and something called 'Webs'. These were long lengths of coarse cloth woven with local wool. The principal customers for this product were the slave owners in the West Indies and Southern States of the USA. The slate industry, not far away up the coast, also increased the need for ships and so the local tradesmen at the yards were kept employed.

By the mid-eighteenth century Y Bermo was also gaining some prominence as a resort and this was greatly enhanced a hundred years later when the

'Cwt y Morwyr' – *the mariners' hut and museum, Bermo*

railway came in 1867. It is recorded that by 1880 the town had five hotels, four inns and as many as one hundred and thirteen lodging houses.

As you step off the ferry one of the first buildings you see is the Lifeboat Museum. It contains a wide assortment of nautical equipment as well as models and of course an 'Honours' corner relating to lifeboat crew members. The museum was set up and is run by the Barmouth Ladies Lifeboat Guild to assist fundraising for the Service. It must be rememberd that the Service is on call permanently, and that crew members are all volunteers.

Nearby is Tŷ Crwn, a circular lock-up built in 1834, Its purpose was to contain drunkern rioters if they became a public nuisance. They would be held here until they could be dealt with by the courts. The building is partitioned down the centre so as to provide accommodation for women as well as men!

The town itself is penned in between the rocky hills

Boats on the Mawddach estuary

immediately behind and the sea. This has led to an interesting jumble of houses perched precariously on rocks and ledges, climbing up the terraces behind the main street. They are accessed by lanes and steps interwoven by paths and alleyways as you proceed up the hillside. We continue on upwards beyond the houses to a minor road and Panorama Walk. Here we can sit on a rocky perch overlooking a magnificent vista which is further enhanced if your visit coincides with the gorse and heather being in full bloom.

Stretched out before you are the dunes of Friog on which you can spot the railway and its station. Before this is Pont y Bermo, stretched like an inert centipede across the estuary. Swing round to your left and cast your eyes over the vast expanse of sea and sand stretching far inland, its flatness emphasised by the mountains crowding in on every shore. Overseeing this, its vast bulk towering on the horizon, is the might of Cadair Idris.

Tŷ Crwn, Y Bermo and the old village

We now return to the sea and cross the estuary by a footpath on the railway bridge. At the time it was built, it posed quite an engineering problem. In fact Afon Mawddach was seen as a major obstacle to the railway builders. It delayed the construction of the railway, for the alternative route circumnavigating the estuary, was a long way round. The very idea of building a viaduct strong enough to carry a train, on sand across the estuary, encouraged many prophets of doom. Nevertheless it is still there, still in use, and still provides a vital rail link between the north and south of the country. On the Bermo side, spanning the deeper channel is a swing bridge, built to allow shipping to pass up into Afon Mawddach. However the coming of the railway brought about, or at least coincided with, a decline in shipping and now it is only the pleasure craft that remind the town of its nautical past.

At the other side of the estuary we reach Morfa

Local heritage on display inside the Tŷ Gwyn on the waterfront

Mawddach Station where we cross reclaimed land to return to the front at Friog.

Walk directions
Start on the front at Friog at any convenient parking point.

1. Either catch the narrow gauge railway or walk to Porth Penrhyn Station on the end of the sandbar. Take the ferry across the estuary. Its operation is to some extent dependent on the tide and checking on this before setting out is advisable. (Try Tourist Information Centre, Y Bermo 01341 280787)

2. Alight from the ferry on the quay (if you wish to explore Y Bermo or visit any of the attractions resume the walk directions at this point.) Follow the quayside to pass under the railway bridge and right on to the A496 towards Dolgellau. Cross the road to the

Bermo harbour bridge

pavement and continue to 'Brambles' restaurant. Just past it take a marked footpath up some brick steps. Climb steeply to a gate and on to a hillside track where you bear right at a T junction. Keep on right over the headland to a fine view over Pont y Bermo and the estuary. Turn inland along a ridge to a gate in a stone wall. Turn left, keeping a wall on your right. The path drops down into a gully between two walls, bear right and follow the path to another gate. Continue with the wall on your right to the next gate. Turn right through it, and go left on to a stone track. Ignore a kissing gate to the right and continue along the track, through a waymarked gate to a junction by a house. Turn left, marked 'TO PANORAMA' and continue through another gate and between stone walls. Then follow a fence on your right. Descend through a gate to a lane and a minor road.

3. Follow the road uphill, past Hafod y Bryn to a gate

The fishermen's quay   *A platform cafe, Y Friog*

on the right marked 'PANORAMA WALK'. The path sweeps right up the hillside and then bears left between two walls. Take a signposted path right through a gate. Follow a clear path through trees to viewpoints over the estuary. Make sure you go as far as the cairn.

4. Return to the minor road and retrace your steps past Hafod y Bryn. Now continue down the road past the footpath which you came up by. You will notice another steep footpath that goes straight down to the road below, when the road itself veers left to circle round on a less precipitous course. Eventually you will meet the A496, the main road out of Y Bermo.

5. Turn right, back towards the town centre, but look out for a footpath left, down to the beginning of Pont y Bermo. Take the toll footbridge, alongside the railway, which runs on to an embankment at the other

Friog station

side. Continue alongside the line as far as Morfa Mawddach Station. At the near end of the platform the line can be crossed to a footpath. This runs along an embankment across the marshes to return you to Friog sea front.

Originally published in
Family Walks to Discover North Wales

by Anna and Graham Francis

Carreg Gwalch Best Valley Walks in Snowdonia

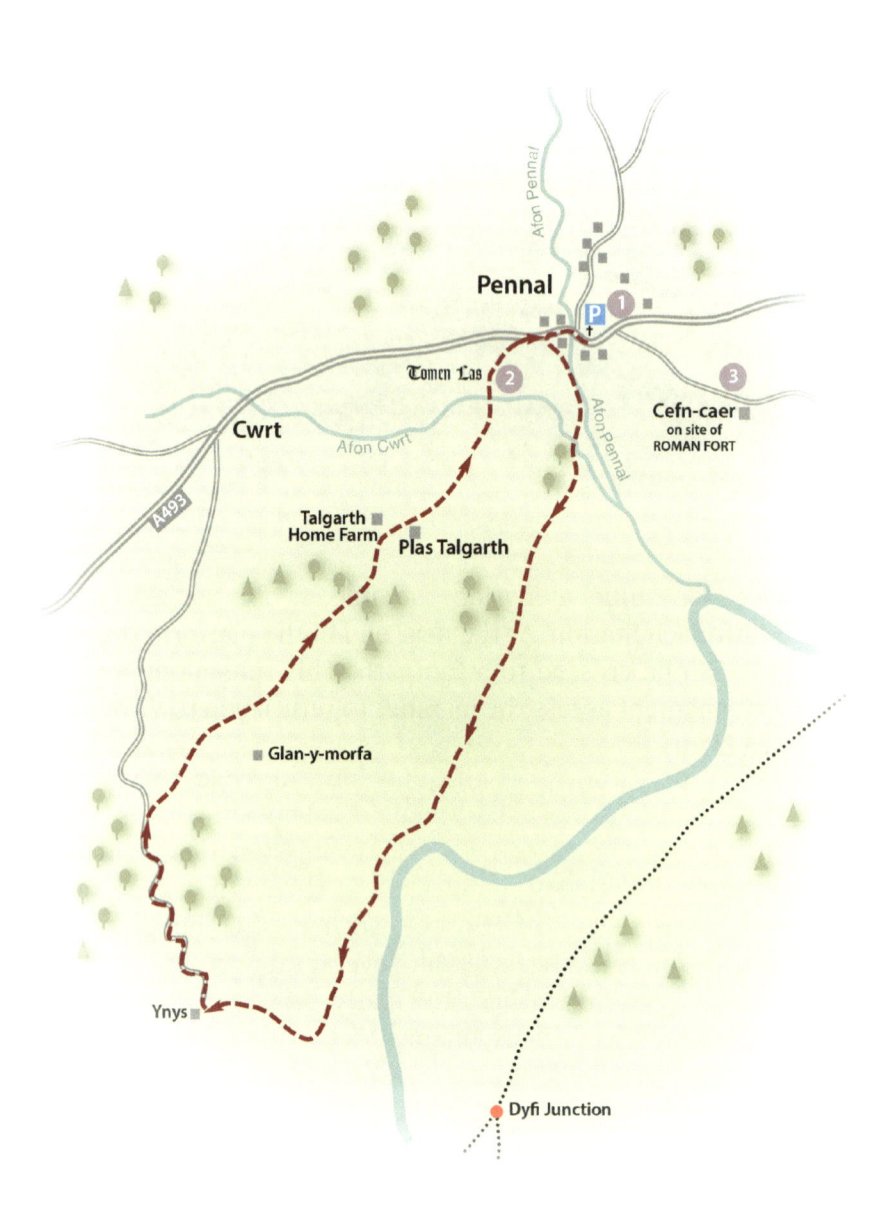

Pennal

Afon Pennal

Cwrt

Tomen Las

Afon Cwrt

A493

Cefn-caer
on site of
ROMAN FORT

Talgarth
Home Farm

Plas Talgarth

Glan-y-morfa

Ynys

Dyfi Junction

Walk 18
Pennal, Dyfi valley

Walk details

Approx distance: 3½ miles/5.8 kilometres

Approx time: 2 hours

O.S. Maps: 1:50 000 *Landranger Sheet 135*
1:25 000 *Explorer OL 23*

Start: *Pennal Church. Grid Reference: SH 699 003*

Access: *Pennal is on the A493, west of Machynlleth. Buses from Machynlleth and Tywyn.*

Parking: *Behind the church by the public toilets.*

Going: *Easy – field, riverside and woodland paths, lanes.*

Points of Interest:

[1] **Pennal church** is the only one in Wales to be dedicated to St Peter ad Vincula (St Peter in Chains). St Tannwg and St Eithrias, Celtic missionaries from Brittany, founded a church here in the sixth century, but it was rededicated by the Normans five hundred years later. It has been rebuilt several times since. The circular churchyard indicates early origins. Although the present church is mainly Victorian, it contains some interesting features, including a 'Green Man' in the East Window. Look for the facsimile of the Pennal Letter sent by Owain Glyndŵr in 1406 to the French King Charles VI. In the letter he pledged allegiance to the French Pope in Avignon – at that time Europe had two Popes – provided certain conditions were met.

Owain Glyndŵr memorial at Pennal church

Cefn Caer farmhouse

Although normally kept in Paris archives, the original letter was loaned to the National Library at Aberystwyth for six months in AD 2000 as part of an exhibition about Owain Glyndŵr's life. Pennal church was Owain Glyndŵr's Chapel Royal in the year 1406 and he may have signed the letter here.

[2] The tree covered mound, **Tomen Las**, is thought to be the site of the medieval court from where Owain Glyndŵr sent the 'Pennal Letter' in 1406.

[3] **Cefn-caer farm** is built in the west corner of the Roman fort. In the field, to the east of the farm, there are signs of foundations in the form of grassy embankments. The fort was sited on Sarn Helen, the Roman road from Caerhun (near Conwy) to *Moridunum* at Caerfyrddin. Roman coins and pottery have been found on the site.

Walk Directions: (–) denotes Point of Interest

1. Face Pennal church [1] and turn left along the A493 to cross the bridge over Afon Pennal. In about 40 metres turn left through a broad gate onto a track.

2. Continue ahead to walk beside the river. Go through a gate across the track. At this point, the track bears right, away from the river. Cross a bridge over a stream and immediately bear right to go through a field gate.

3. Slant left to reach a stream and continue through the field with the ditch on your right. Pass alongside woodland. When you reach the end of the field go through a small gate and cross a ladder stile.

4. Walk on beside the stream until you reach a footbridge across it. Cross and turn left. In a few metres, veer slightly right to follow another ditch on your right.

5. On reaching the end of the field, cross a boggy ditch then climb to the top of an embankment and turn right to cross a stile. Afon Dyfi is now on your left. Walk along the embankment and ignore a stile below on the right.

6. Look for a footbridge on the right and, after crossing it, walk ahead with a ditch on the left. Before reaching the end of the field, go through a gate on your

left. Walk along the fence on your right to a gate straight ahead. Turn left and walk towards the farmhouse. Go through a gate to the right of it.

7. Walk up to the lane and follow it uphill. Ignore a track on the left. Continue along the undulating lane. Pass some houses, a track to Penmaenbach, and a bungalow on the left.

8. When the lane descends, cross a stile near a gate on the right. Walk up the field and, at the top of a knoll, go through a gate. Bear slightly left, then right, to pass between buildings.

9. Walk ahead and go through a gate into a field. Continue ahead uphill towards woodland – from here there are fine views of the estuary.

10. On reaching a fence, go through a kissing gate into a strip of woodland. A clear path goes slightly downhill and, in a few metres, has a fence on the right.

11. Follow the path as it levels then goes slightly uphill to a stile. Continue beside the fence and cross a stile into a wood. In a few metres, ignore a path on the left, and walk ahead. On joining a wider path, turn left.

12. The path emerges at the Plas Talgarth holiday complex. Walk ahead to reach the access drive and continue along it to a

junction. Turn left to follow a lane between fields which leads to the A493.

13. After crossing a stream, you will see the mound, Tomen Las [2] on your right. On reaching the A493, turn right to return to the church in Pennal.

Plas Talgarth

14. If you have time to spare, and would like to see the site of the Roman fort at Pennal, continue along the A493 for about 100 metres, then turn right along a lane. Follow it for about 600 metres, to just beyond the farm of Cefn-caer [3].

Facilities:
Refreshments at the Riverside Hotel. Public toilets behind the church.

Originally published in
Circular Walks in the Dyfi Valley

by Dorothy Hamilton

Afon Mawddach
Penmaenpool Bridge
P
1
Penmaenpool Morfa Mawddach Walk
George III Hotel
A493
Penmaenpool
Abergwynant
Woods
2
3
4
5
6
7
Cae'n y Coed
Afon Gwynant

Walk 19
Penmaenpool

Walk details

Approx distance: 5 miles/8 kilometres

Approx time: About 3 hours

O.S. Maps: 1:50 000 *Landranger Sheet 124*
1:25 000 *Explorer OL 23*

Start: Car park near the Barmouth toll bridge at Penmaenpool.
Grid Ref. SH 695 186

Access: *Penmaenpool is on the A493, west of Dolgellau. Buses from Dolgellau, Machynlleth, Aberystwyth and Tywyn. When in Penmaenpool follow signs for the Barmouth toll bridge.*

Parking: *Car park near the George III Hotel and toll bridge in Penmaenpool. Toilet facilities are available.*

Please note: *Moderate – forest, moorland, fields, lane and estuary track bed of old railway.*

Going: *This walk starts by following the old railway track beside Afon Mawddach. After this level stretch, the route climbs gradually into the hills, from where there are superb views.*

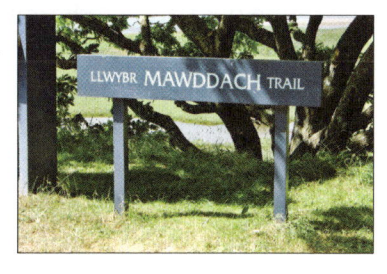

This lovely walk starts by following an easy, level stretch of the **Mawddach Trail**, a walking and cycling route from Barmouth to Dolgellau. It follows the track bed of the Ruabon-Barmouth railway line which closed in 1965 after operating for one hundred years. It opened to bring Victorian visitors to the Cambrian coast and transported slate and copper from the local quarries.

The **George III Hotel** in Penmaenpool (Pwll Penmaen) was built in 1650, and was originally two buildings; an inn, and a ship chandlers. The whole area was a centre for boat building, with many of the inlets along the Mawddach having boatyards, making sloops of oak from the local woodlands. All this activity ceased with the coming of the railways in the mid-19th century. The line only operated for about 100 years before closing in 1965. The old signal box Is an RSPB centre. Lapwings, shelduck, common sandpiper, red-breasted merganser, curlew, heron and cormorants may be spotted with the binoculars, available for public use, at the centre. The nearby toll bridge, over the head of the Mawddach, was built in 1879 and could be opened for the passage of

ships. Gerard Manley Hopkins stayed at the George III Hotel and wrote a poem about Penmaenpool:
>'O where live well your lease of leisure
>But here at, here at Penmaenpool.'

Many species of birds can be spotted from the track such as heron, cormorant, common sandpiper and red-breasted merganser. It is worthwhile to carry binoculars. From higher sections of the walk there are superb views of the estuary as well as the **Aran mountains** and **Cadair Idris** range.

Walk Directions

1. From the car park, walk towards the toll bridge and pass the signal box. Continue along the old railway track beside Afon Mawddach, passing the George III Hotel. Go through a kissing-gate and continue along the track. Ignore a little gate on the left at picnic tables and walk on beside Abergwynant Woods. Pass more picnic tables on the left and a reedy area, with outcrops behind it, on the left. Ahead of you is a level bridge. A few paces before reaching it, go left on a wide track, passing around a gate.

2. Ignore a track on the left and go ahead with a small river on your right. Further on, there is a field to your right. When the track veers right, go through a gate into the field and follow the track to another gate where it meets a drive coming from a house on the left. Go ahead, with Afon Gwynant on your right, and ignore a bridge across it. Pass Abergwynant Farm and walk along the lane,

through tall trees to the A493.

3. Cross the road with care. Turn left, then right along a lane. Follow it around bends uphill with views of a ravine below on the right. Pass trees, then a field, on your left. When the field ends, go left on a track, passing a house (Cae'n-y-Coed) on your right. When the main track bends left to a house, leave it to go ahead on another track to a gate. To the left of it there is a ladder stile.

4. Follow the track around bends, uphill, pausing now and again to look back at the views. Further on, you will have a wall on the left. Continue along the track and pass a scree covered hill on your right. After the end of the scree, and before the track reaches a wall corner, go left a few paces on a narrow path to a stone step stile in a wall. It has a post with a yellow arrow on it.

5. Go slightly left and over a rise then downhill.

The path veers to the left to pass another scree covered hill and wall on the right. Ignore a small gate and follow a fence on the right to a ladder stile. Continue downhill along the right side of the field, passing trees. Go through a gap into the next field, to bear right over a stream.

6. Go ahead on a grassy track with great views of the surrounding mountains. When the track reaches a tree a few metres before a stone building, go left downhill to the corner of the field and go through a right-hand metal gate near farm buildings. Pass a stone building on your right, then go left through a gate and follow a building, passes it on the left and then winds downhill with a wood on the left, before slanting right to join another track coming from a house.

7. Turn left and, when the track bends right, leave it to go ahead through trees to a ladder stile. Descend the narrow path through scrub and small trees to emerge on a track on the right. Just before reaching a house, go through a gate on the right with a yellow arrow. Pass the side of the house on your left and follow the path downhill to the A493. Cross with care and turn right to the car park and start of the walk.

Originally published in
Short Family Walks in Snowdonia

by Dorothy Hamilton

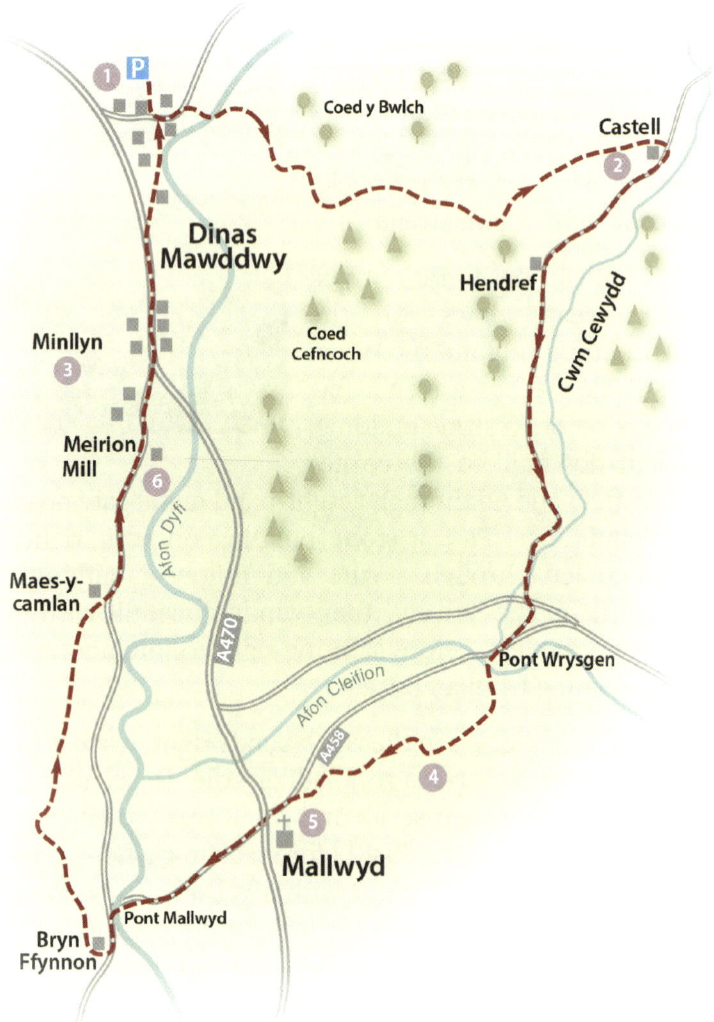
P
Coed y Bwlch
Castell
Dinas
Mawddwy
Hendref
Cwm Cewydd
Minllyn
Coed
Cefncoch
Meirion
Mill
Afon Dyfi
Maes-y-
camlan
A470
Pont Wrysgen
Afon Cleifion
A458
Mallwyd
Pont Mallwyd
Bryn
Ffynnon
1
2
3
4
5
6

Walk 20
Cwm Cewydd, Dinas Mawddwy

Walk details

Approx distance: 6½ miles/10.5 kilometres

Approx time: About 4 hours

O.S. Maps: 1:50 000 *Landranger Sheet* 124
1:25 000 *Explorer OL* 23

Start: *Gwesty'r Llew Coch (The Red Lion) in Dinas Mawddwy. Grid Reference: SH 858 148.*

Access: *Dinas Mawddwy is just off the A470, 10 miles (16 km) east of Dolgellau. Infrequent buses from Machynlleth and Dolgellau.*

Parking: *As you approach the crossroad junction by Gwesty'r Llew Coch, cross the road to a car park near a play park on the opposite side.*

Going: *Moderate – woodland and hillside paths, tracks and lanes.*

Points of Interest:

[1] During the 15th and 16th centuries, Dinas Mawddwy was the territory of **Gwylliaid Cochion Mawddwy** (the *Red Bandits of Mawddwy*). Such was their notoriety, travellers crossed mountains on their journeys rather than take the road. Houses in the neighbourhood were built with a scythe-blade pointing skywards in the chimneys to deter the bandits from entering from the roofs. They were called Red Bandits because most of them had red hair. They stole cattle and sheep and terrorised everyone. In 1554, Sir John

Wynn of Gwydir and Baron Lewis Owen of Dolgellau were authorised to punish them. On Christmas Eve of that year they caught more than eighty of the bandits and all were condemned to death. The mother of two of them begged Baron Owen to spare the life of her youngest son. When he refused, she screamed and tore her blouse to reveal her breasts and said 'These breasts have given suck to those who shall wash their hands in your blood'. In the following year, Baron Owen was ambushed by the remaining bandits. All those with the baron fled except for his son-in-law, John Llwyd. It is said that the remaining sons of the old woman dipped their hands in his blood. After the baron's death the outlaws were completely exterminated. Dinas Mawddwy became an important centre for lead mining and slate quarrying.

[2] **Castell** is said to have a ghost. A woman who owned this farmhouse had an unfaithful husband. When she died, he forged her will using her dead hand. Later, the ghost of a hand was seen and there were other weird activities including furniture shaking and strange sounds.

[3] Over one hundred men worked at the **Minllyn slate quarry** before it closed about 1916. Tramways took the product to a mill on the valley floor. There are some interesting remains on the site, including the ruined mill, workshops, chimney and a tramway that goes through a tunnel to a pit.

[4] It is said that the Red Bandits of Mawddwy were buried near Collfryn, which is just over two kilometres south-east of this point. The lane on your left leads to Gweinion, and continues as a track and a right-of-way. After fording a stream, it goes uphill to a fork. The left-hand track descends towards Colfryn. Before the

cottage, at the eastern boundary of the wood on the left, is a large tree covered mound reputed to be the burial place of the bandits. Although not a right-of-way, use of the track is usually permitted to view the burial ground.

[5] **St Tydecho** was a missionary from Brittany and he founded a church on this site in the sixth century. The present building dates from the 14th century and has dormer windows at different levels. Inside are tiered pews and a barrel roof. Above the porch, dated 1641 are prehistoric animal bones which were dug up nearby about 1850. The **Brigands Inn** is said to have been the meeting place of the Red Bandits of Mawddwy. George Borrow stayed at the inn: he thought Mallwyd an attractive village.

[6] **Meirion woollen mill** is located in the old station

The Brigands' Inn

of the former Mawddwy Railway. It ran from Cemaes Road (Glantwymyn) from 1868 to 1951. The coffee shop used to be the station master's house and booking office. Nearby is a 17th century double arched packhorse bridge known as Pont Minllyn.

Walk Directions: (–) **denotes Point of Interest**

1. From the Y Llew Coch (*The Red Lion*) in Dinas Mawddwy [1] take the minor road signposted Llanymawddwy. Walk downhill and in about 100 metres turn right on a clear track.

2. Cross a footbridge over Afon Dyfi and, with the

Y Llew Coch, Dinas Mawddwy

river on your left, follow a path to a kissing gate. Immediately bear right and pass through a gap which once had a gate onto an enclosed track. After going through a wooden gate, bear right beside a fence. Pass through a metal gate and emerge on a track.

3. Turn right along the track and pass a house on the left. In about another 100 metres, where the track bears right, leave it to go ahead through a gate. Walk up to a footpath signpost then bear left to follow a fence on your left. Cross a stile into the wood and continue beside the fence. In about 15 metres turn right on a clear and steep path, uphill.

4. At the top of the wood climb over a stile and cross the field diagonally left. Go through trees to cross the field boundary and in about 10 metres follow an old river course to a stile in a fence on the left. Cross the stile then bear right along an old track. On reaching a corner, veer left on the track to have a wood on your right. As you climb higher there are lovely views across the Dyfi valley to Cwm Cywarch and the Aran Mountains.

5. Continue along the track and pass through a number of gates. After a left bend it descends to have views of Cwm Cewydd on the right. Ignore the stile on

your right. Continue ahead and go through another gate then, at the track junction, bear right to a metal gate. Pass farm buildings on your left and a fantastic view of Cwm Cewydd on your right. Walk downhill to emerge on a lane.

6. Turn right past Castell [2] and continue along the lane passing Fferm yr Hendre (or Hendref on the OS map) on your right. In 1.5 kilometres ignore an access lane on the right (GR 872 136). Continue walking down the lane, crossing a bridge then to a lane junction. Turn left for a few metres then bear right on another lane that descends to the A458. Take care as you will now need to walk along the A458 which is a main road. At the junction, turn right and in about 50 metres cross a bridge over Afon Cleifion. Cross the road to a stile at the end of the bridge. Climb over the stile.

7. Descend to walk along with the river on your left. In about 100 metres, leave the river to bear right uphill through trees to a field. Slant left to a fence but do not go through the metal gate to which is ahead. With the fence on your left, walk uphill. After passing through more trees, continue uphill to a corner fence. Bear right and, at the end of the fence, join a track.

8. Turn right along the track and follow it to a metal gate. From here you can look across the Dyfi valley to the remains of Minllyn quarry [3] above Coed Foeldinas. Emerge on an access lane [4] and bear right, downhill.

9. The lane descends to the A458. (A few metres to the right there is a cafe at the Murco garage.) Turn left to Brigands Inn and the roundabout with the A470. About 100 metres to the left stands the interesting 14th century church dedicated to St Tydecho [5]. At the roundabout, cross to the minor road opposite (second exit from A458) to Pont Mallwyd.

10. Follow the lane to Pont Mallwyd spanning Afon Dyfi. Ignore the footpath sign and stile on your left before crossing the bridge. Cross the bridge then turn left for about 100 metres. Immediately after passing the garden of a house called Bryn Ffynnon on your right, and opposite a track on your left, go through a gate on your right with the "Llwybr Cyhoeddus" (*Public Footpath*) sign.

11. Walk ahead on a track and follow it when it bears right to another gate. Walk uphill and, at a fork, ignore a track on the right. Continue uphill and at the next fork, bear right to cross a stream at a ford.
N.B. You may come across many pheasants along this path; this is due to a pheasant farm nearby. Take care when walking this trail as they do fly low in all directions.

12. Climb a ladder stile and, with the Dyfi valley below on your right, walk across the field. Descend slightly to a stile. With a fence on your right, walk ahead. This

field is known as Maes-y-camlan, and is one of the many sites attributed to where King Arthur is said to have fought his last battle against Mordred.

13. At the end of the fence, pass through a gate. Immediately bear right to go through more gates and pass farm buildings on the right. Emerge on a lane and turn left.

14. In about 550 metres, after the lane crosses a stream, a path on the right leads to Meirion Mill [6]. Continue along the lane to the A470. If you visit the mill, leave by the exit onto the main road. Turn left along the A470 and continue for about 300 metres. Bear right along a road signposted for Dinas Mawddwy. It leads to the Gwesty'r Llew Coch (*The Red Lion*) and the start of the walk.

Facilities:
Refreshments at Gwesty'r Llew Coch, Mallwyd and Meirion Mill. Public toilets are opposite Gwesty'r Llew Coch at the start. Camp sites nearby.

Originally published in
Circular Walks in the Dyfi Valley

by Dorothy Hamilton

Walk 21
Aberllefenni, Afon Dulas, Corris

Walk details

Approx distance: 7 miles/11.5 kilometres

Approx time: About 4 hours.

O.S. Maps: 1:50 000 *Landranger Sheet 124 or Landranger 135*
1:25 000 *Explorer OL 23 or Explorer 215*

Start: *Car park at the Corris Railway Museum.*
Grid Reference: SH 754 078

Access: *Corris is off the A487, north of Machynlleth. At the Braich Goch Hotel, turn right into Corris village. Buses from Dolgellau and Machynlleth.*

Parking: *Signposted parking at Corris Railway Museum.*

Going: *Moderate – riverside and forest paths, tracks and lanes.*

Points of Interest:

[1] **Corris** lies in the steep valley of Afon Dulas, surrounded by the remains of slate quarrying. The extraction of slate has been the chief factor in the development of the village, although forestry is now the main industry in the area. The planting of the Dyfi forest began in 1926. The Roman road Sarn Helen passed this way and the Romans may have quarried slate in the area. In 1859, a horse-drawn tramway connected the quarries around Corris with the port at Derwen-las on the Dyfi. When the Cambrian Railway opened in 1867, the tramway west of Machynlleth became disused. Steam engines were introduced on

the Corris Railway line in 1879 and, for a short while, there was a passenger service. The quarries continued to use the line until 1948, when flood damage to the Dyfi Bridge forced its closure. Braich Goch, the largest quarry in Corris, employing about two hundred men, was sited north-east of the village. Since closure in 1971, the area has been landscaped and the main road actually crosses the mill area.

[2] Still in use, the **Aberllefenni quarry** has probably been worked since the 16th century. It produces very high quality slate. The underground workings were connected to the mill by a tramway which was in use until the 1970s. The terminus of the Corris railway was opposite the mill. Remains of the railway can be seen at various places in the valley.

Walk Directions: (–) **denotes Point of Interest**
1. From the car park walk out to the road and bear right through Corris [1]. After crossing Afon Deri, turn right on a lane downhill. Cross Afon Dulas and follow the lane as it bears right. Continue past houses and walk uphill. Pass a track on the right to Fronfelin Hall.

2. In about 100 metres, when the lane starts to descend, turn left on a path that rises into the forest. Ignore a signposted track on the left and continue ahead to reach a wider track.

3. Bear left and, on reaching a fork, go right to continue on the wide track. Take care as motocross

bikes also use this trail. Walk ahead for 670 metres until you reach a footpath signpost on the right. The trail ascends through forest until you come to a wide track at a crossroad.

4. At the crossroad, walk straight ahead (east/north-east) along the wide track. On your right (south-east) there are fantastic views of Cwm Glesyrch stretching to Dyffryn Dyfi and beyond. Continue ahead for about 500 metres to a fork and bear left.

5. Keep to the wide track which bends to the right and continues for a kilometre until you reach a gate. Cross this gate and proceed to follow the trail along Mynydd Esgairneiriau. Be wary of any cattle in the fields. Cross a cattle grid and continue pass a derelict farm building on your right – 'Esgairneiriau'.

6. On this track you can see to the east that on the side of a mountain is a large hole which was the entrance to underground slate workings. The track bends to the left and in about 100 metres leave the trail by going downhill through the field on your left. Bear right (west) to a wooden gate at the edge of the wood.

7. Go through the gate and follow the woodland trail downhill. Take care as the path can be slippery due to small streams flowing to Afon Dulas. After walking almost 700 metres the trail bends to the right. At this point there is a small trail on your left leading to a wooden bridge that crosses Nant Esgair-neiriau. Cross the bridge and follow the riverside trail.

8. In about 300 metres there will be a ruin on your right, turn right to cross a stile and walk downhill along the side of the field. At the bottom, bear left to follow a fence above Afon Dulas. Go through a gate on the right into trees, and walk downhill on a wide track. Emerge in a field and walk ahead.

9. Climb over a stile near a gate and cross a footbridge over Afon Dulas. Go through some gates and pass a farm building on the left. Follow the farm drive but, before it reaches the lane, bear left to cross an old bridge.

10. Go up some steps to the lane and turn left. Aberllefenni quarries are on the right [2].

11. Continue along the road and pass the slate mill on the left and houses on the right. Immediately beyond the road sign for Aberllefenni, turn left downhill into a Forestry picnic site and car park.

12. When the track turns left, continue on a gravel path to have Afon Dulas on the left. On reaching a track, turn left to cross a bridge over the river. Immediately turn right on a track.

Aberllefenni Slate Quarry as seen from Esgairneiriau

13. Cross a bridge over a small stream and bear right to a telegraph pole. Walk along a path to pass the garden of the house on the left. Go through a small gate into a field.

14. Walk beside Afon Dulas. Notice the slate in the river. Continue ahead through the fields, crossing stiles. When the last field narrows, walk ahead on a path through woodland, beside the river.

15. Climb over a stile and continue on a clear path some distance from the river. Cross a stream by stepping stones and a fence type stile. Walk through a field by keeping slightly uphill from the river. Pass a small gate on the left and cross a stream. Maintain your direction to reach a broad gate, and enter woodland.

16. Continue ahead on a clear track. Go uphill to join another track. Bear right to pass above a quarry. Go through a broad gate and continue ahead.

17. Emerge on a lane and turn right to retrace your steps into Corris and the start of the walk.

Facilities:
Alternative parking at the Forestry Picnic Site near Aberllefenni. Public toilets near the start. Railway museum. Corris Railway. Cafe at Corris Craft Centre on the A487. King Arthur's Labyrinth. Youth hostel in Corris.

Originally published in
Circular Walks in the Dyfi Valley

by Dorothy Hamilton

Best Walks in Wales

A series of guide books to take you to every corner of this magnificent walking country

- **Short family walks**
- **Excellent coastal walks**
- **Hill and mountain walks & panoramic views**
- **Level lakeside and valley walks**
- **Woodland and nature walks**
- **Fascinating heritage and history guides**
- **Clear coloured maps**
- **Route photos and attractions on the way**
- **Updated directions**

www.carreg-gwalch.com

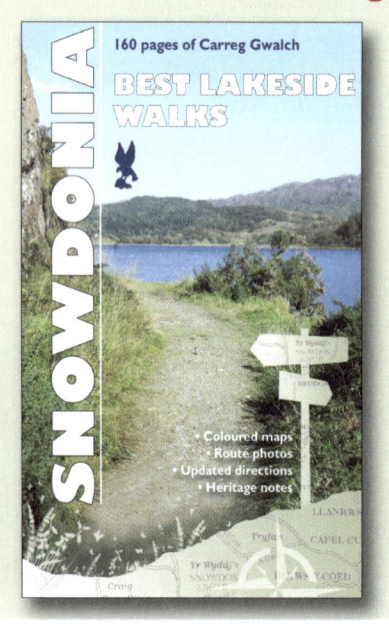

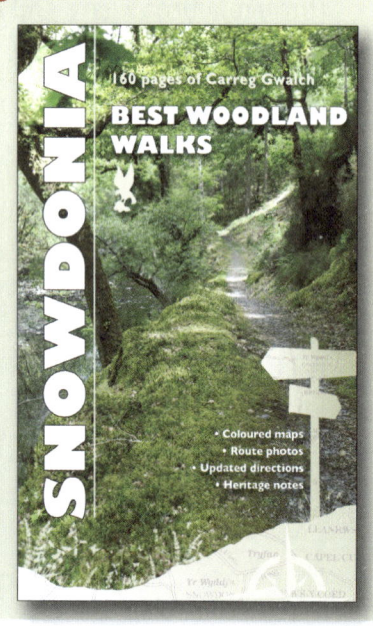

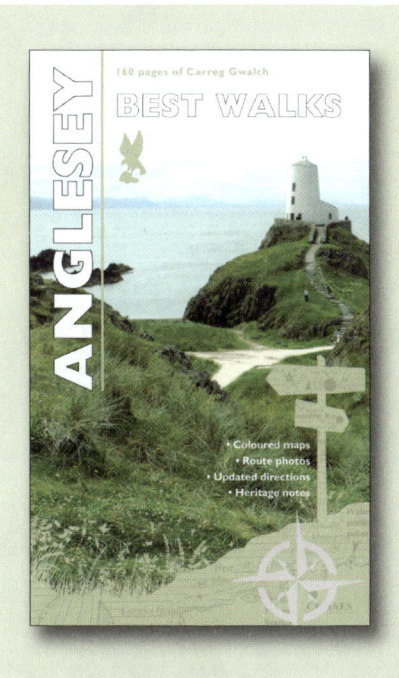

ANGLESEY BEST WALKS

160 pages of Carreg Gwalch

- Coloured maps
- Route photos
- Updated directions
- Heritage notes

LLŶN BEST WALKS

160 pages of Carreg Gwalch

- Coloured maps
- Route photos
- Updated directions
- Heritage notes

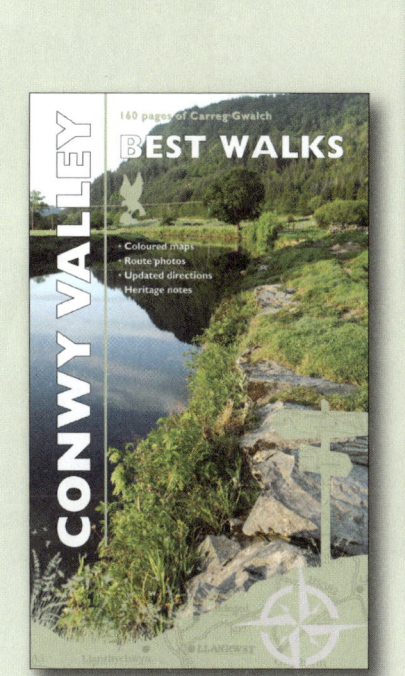

CONWY VALLEY BEST WALKS

160 pages of Carreg Gwalch

- Coloured maps
- Route photos
- Updated directions
- Heritage notes

CENTRAL WALES
160 pages of Carreg Gwalch
BEST WALKS
• Coloured maps
• Route photos
• Updated directions
• Heritage notes
BEACON MOUNTAINS
160 pages of Carreg Gwalch
BEST WALKS
PEMBROKESHIRE
160 pages of Carreg Gwalch
BEST WALKS
• Coloured maps
• Route photos
• Updated directions
• Heritage notes
CLWYDIAN RANGE
160 pages of Carreg Gwalch
BEST WALKS
• Coloured maps
• Route photos
• Updated directions
• Heritage notes
GLAMORGAN & GWENT
• Coloured maps
• Route photos
• Updated directions
• Heritage notes